UNDERSTANDING THE HOLOCAUST

D1266020

Holocaust Rescue and Liberation

Craig E. Blohm

ReferencePoint Press®

San Diego, CA

About the Author

Craig E. Blohm has written numerous books and magazine articles for young readers. He and his wife, Desiree, reside in Tinley Park, Illinois.

© 2016 ReferencePoint Press, Inc.
Printed in the United States

For more information, contact:
ReferencePoint Press, Inc.
PO Box 27779
San Diego, CA 92198
www.ReferencePointPress.com

LIBRARY OF CONGRESS CATALOGING-IN-PUBLICATION DATA

Blohm, Craig E., 1948- author
  Holocaust rescue and liberation / by Craig E. Blohm.
    pages cm. -- (Understanding the Holocaust series)
  Includes bibliographical references and index.
  ISBN-13: 978-1-60152-844-5 (hardback)
  ISBN-10: 1-60152-844-2 (hardback)
  1. World War, 1939-1945--Jews--Rescue--Juvenile literature. 2. Righteous Gentiles in the Holocaust--Juvenile literature. 3. Holocaust, Jewish (1939-1945)--Juvenile literature. I. Title.
  D804.34.B56 2016
  940.53'1835--dc23
                                                         2015016547

CONTENTS

1937
Buchenwald concentration camp is established in east-central Germany.

1941
Germany invades the Soviet Union; the Germans massacre about one hundred thousand Jews, Roma (Gypsies), Communists, and others at Babi Yar in Ukraine; the United States declares war on Japan and Germany after Japan attacks Pearl Harbor.

1920
The Nazi Party publishes its 25-point program declaring its intention to segregate Jews from so-called Aryan society and to eliminate the political, legal, and civil rights of Germany's Jewish population.

1925
Adolf Hitler's autobiographical manifesto *Mein Kampf* is published; in it he outlines his political ideology and future plans for Germany and calls for the violent elimination of the world's Jews.

1940
The Warsaw ghetto—a 1.3 square mile (3.4 sq km) area sealed off from the rest of the city by high walls, barbed wire, and armed guards—is established in Poland.

1920 / 1934 1936 1938 1940

1918
The Treaty of Versailles, marking the formal end of World War I and a humiliating defeat for Germany, is signed.

1935
The Nuremberg Laws, excluding German Jews from citizenship and depriving them of the right to vote and hold public office, are enacted.

1939
Germany invades Poland, igniting World War II in Europe; in Warsaw, Jews are forced to wear white armbands with a blue Star of David.

1933
Hitler is appointed Germany's chancellor; the Gestapo is formed; Dachau concentration camp is established.

1938
Violent anti-Jewish attacks known as *Kristallnacht* (Night of Broken Glass) take place throughout greater Germany; the first *Kindertransport* (children's transport) arrives in Great Britain with thousands of Jewish children seeking refuge from Nazi persecution.

1942
The Nazi plan to annihilate Europe's Jews (the Final Solution) is outlined at the Wannsee Conference in Berlin; deportations of about 1.5 million Jews to killing centers in Poland begin.

1944
Allied forces carry out the D-Day invasion at Normandy in France; diplomats in Budapest offer protection to Jews.

1948
The State of Israel is established as a homeland for the world's Jews.

1946
The International Military Tribunal imposes death and prison sentences during the Nuremberg Trials.

1949
Argentina grants asylum to Josef Mengele, the notorious SS doctor who performed medical experiments on prisoners in Auschwitz.

1942   1944   1946   1948 / 1970

1943
Despite armed Jewish resistance, the Nazis move to liquidate ghettos in Poland and the Soviet Union; Denmark actively resists Nazi attempts to deport its Jewish citizens.

1960
In Argentina, Israeli intelligence agents abduct Adolf Eichmann, one of the masterminds of the Holocaust; he is brought to Israel to stand trial for crimes against the Jewish people.

1945
Allied forces liberate Auschwitz, Buchenwald, and Dachau concentration camps; Hitler commits suicide; World War II ends with the surrender of Germany and Japan; the Nuremberg Trials begin with war crimes indictments against leading Nazis.

1981
More than ten thousand survivors attend the first World Gathering of Jewish Holocaust Survivors in Israel; a similar gathering two years later in Washington, DC, attracts twenty thousand people.

1947
The UN General Assembly adopts a resolution partitioning Palestine into Jewish and Arab states; Holocaust survivor Simon Wiesenthal opens a center in Austria to search for Nazis who have evaded justice.

The Courage of the Rescuers

On January 30, 1933, Adolf Hitler became chancellor of Germany, a nation devastated by its defeat in World War I followed by the worldwide Great Depression that had begun in 1929. The German people saw Hitler as a desperately needed savior who promised to restore Germany to the powerful nation it once had been. "I will employ my strength for the welfare of the German people," he declared, "and conduct my affairs of office impartially and with justice to everyone."[1] A skilled and passionate orator, Hitler's speeches were met with wild cheers and shouts of "Heil Hitler!"

As Hitler and his Nazi Party gained more power, a more sinister political agenda emerged: the extermination of the Jewish people. Hitler's hatred of Jews went back to his days as a disenchanted youth in Austria. When Germany lost World War I, he blamed Jews for the defeat. Now that he wielded nearly absolute power in Germany, he could act on his anti-Semitic beliefs. In 1935 Germany passed the Nuremberg Laws, which stripped Jews of their German citizenship and prohibited marriage between Jews and non-Jews. Soon even more restrictive laws were enacted. By World War II Jews were being herded into concentration camps where they were worked to death or murdered in gas chambers.

Bystanders

In Germany and the German-occupied territories of Europe, signs of Jewish persecution could be seen if one knew where to look. Every morning, Jewish inmates of the Dachau concentration camp were marched by their Nazi captors through the streets of the town to work as slave laborers in a nearby armaments factory. From storefronts and apartment windows, citizens of Dachau silently watched the daily procession pass by, knowing where the prisoners were headed but never reacting. In the Polish town of Auschwitz, the air was filled day and night with the stench of the crematoria as the bodies of gassed Jews were burned. Flames emanating from the camp's smokestacks could be seen by anyone who cared to look. But the people of Auschwitz remained silent. Freight trains rumbled through the countryside with their cargo of Jews jammed in like cattle. No one protested.

Most German citizens were naturally preoccupied with daily life in a time of war, dealing with food shortages and concerned with loved ones at the battlefront. Many denied that atrocities were taking place, believing that such reports were merely Allied propaganda. Still many others who comprehended what was really going on simply looked the other way as the Nazis slaughtered innocent Jews and others deemed unworthy of living. It is perhaps not difficult to understand why: The penalty for hiding Jews or helping them escape was death or imprisonment in a concentration camp. Martin Wittmann, a resident of the town of Dachau, was interviewed by a member of the US military after liberation of the Dachau concentration camp; he stated simply, "It was all very horrible, but what could we do?"[2] During the course of the war, that question was resoundingly answered by the actions of countless men and women who risked their lives to rescue Jews.

The Rescuers

Thousands of ordinary people from all walks of life felt compelled to do something in response to the atrocities committed by the Nazis. Many provided a refuge in their home where individuals or even entire families could hide from the Nazis. Others created false identity documents so that Jews could flee Germany to the safety of neutral nations. Smuggling food and weapons into overcrowded ghettos, spiriting children away from danger in the middle of the night, and building camps in the deep forests where Jews could hide and help partisans fight the Nazis were all part of a vast effort to help the oppressed Jews. The rescuers included individuals such as Corrie ten Boom, who opened her home in the Netherlands to Jewish refugees, or groups such as the Polish underground resistance organization Zegota. In at least one case, the people of an entire country, Denmark, came together to aid in the escape of Jews to Sweden.

In some instances the rescuers knew the people they helped. In other instances they did not. In either case years later the question arose: Why would some people risk everything to aid the Jews while others stood idly by? Compassion, empathy, and opportunity were strong motivators whether rescuers worked in the helping professions (such as health care) or in government or business. Most rescuers were ordinary people who, despite the danger, helped someone in need. "I did nothing special," declares a Polish rescuer, "and I don't consider myself a hero. I simply acted on my human obligation to the persecuted and suffering."[3]

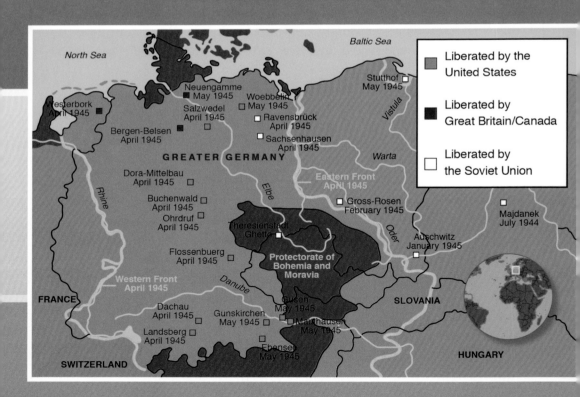

The Liberation of Major Nazi Camps, 1944–1945

North Sea

Baltic Sea

Liberated by the United States

Liberated by Great Britain/Canada

Liberated by the Soviet Union

Westerbork
April 1945

Neuengamme
May 1945

Woebbelin
May 1945

Stutthof
May 1945

Salzwedel
April 1945

Ravensbrück
April 1945

Bergen-Belsen
April 1945

Sachsenhausen
April 1945

GREATER GERMANY

Warta

Dora-Mittelbau
April 1945

Eastern Front
April 1945

Gross-Rosen
February 1945

Majdanek
July 1944

Buchenwald
April 1945

Ohrdruf
April 1945

Theresienstadt
Ghetto

Auschwitz
January 1945

Flossenburg
April 1945

Protectorate of
Bohemia and
Moravia

Western Front
April 1945

Danube

FRANCE

SLOVANIA

Dachau
April 1945

Gunskirchen
May 1945

Gusen
May 1945

Mauthausen
May 1945

Landsberg
April 1945

Ebensee
May 1945

HUNGARY

SWITZERLAND

Vistula

Rhine

Elbe

Oder

8

Uncovering the Truth

While the rescuers continued to perform their courageous actions throughout the war, the *Wehrmacht* (German armed forces) was fighting on two fronts, a situation that ensured its ultimate defeat. The end for Germany began as the Soviet Red Army pushed German soldiers westward while US and British forces advanced toward the east. In July 1944 Soviet troops came upon Majdanek concentration camp near Lublin, Poland, the first Nazi camp to be liberated. The Nazis had abandoned the camp, leaving behind evidence of their atrocities: gas chambers, mass graves, and about a thousand barely surviving inmates. Photographs and reports of the camp began appearing in Soviet newspapers and were later reprinted in Western news media. Soviet forces continued their march through Nazi territory, liberating concentration camps and killing centers at Sachsenhausen, Ravensbrück, and Auschwitz. US and British forces reached Buchenwald, Dachau, and Bergen-Belsen. In April 1945 soldiers

> "I did nothing special, and I don't consider myself a hero. I simply acted on my human obligation to the persecuted and suffering."[3]
>
> —Polish rescuer.

with the US Fourth Armored Division entered Ohrdruf, a subcamp of the Buchenwald concentration camp in central Germany. They discovered piles of partially incinerated bodies. When word of the horrors reached General Dwight D. Eisenhower, he visited the camp. As he later wrote in his memoir of the war, at Ohrdruf, Eisenhower "came face to face with indisputable evidence of Nazi brutality and ruthless disregard of every shred of decency."[4] He called for widespread press coverage of the evidence of war crimes committed there and forced local citizens to tour the camp to view firsthand what the Nazis had done. The world's newspapers and newsreel films soon brought the horrors of the Holocaust to a mass audience.

For those who denied that the Holocaust actually happened, as well as for those who looked the other way, the early postwar period was one of discovery, admission, and shame. For those who had braved the dangers of an evil regime to help people who were mercilessly persecuted, it was a time to return to their normal lives. Their courageous acts of rescue would eventually be told in books, films, and in thousands of speeches given in schools, churches, and assembly halls. Like the Holocaust itself, the rescuers will never be forgotten.

CHAPTER ONE

Sheltering the Jews

Felix Zandman tore the yellow Star of David patches from his coat and quietly walked away from his job outside the ghetto where he lived in Grodno, Poland. It was February 12, 1943, and the fifteen-year-old had just learned that the ghetto was surrounded by German soldiers. Zandman knew what that meant: a roundup of Jews and deportation to the dreaded concentration camps. Seeking shelter, he headed for the nearby Lososna Forest where his family once owned some small summer cottages. Although the cottages were now gone, the former caretakers, a couple named Jan and Anna Puchalski, still lived nearby. Zandman planned to spend the night with them and then join the partisans in the forest. But the Puchalskis had a different idea, as Zandman recalled in 1986:

> When I appeared at their house, they received me with great warmth, gave me something to eat, and afterwards asked me to agree to stay with them. . . . The Puchalskis offered to hide me until the end of the war. I did not have any money, not even a watch, to offer them. They were extremely poor. Everyone was hungry there, yet they offered to share with me what they had.[5]

The Puchalskis dug a bunker beneath their house and hid Zandman and three other Jews there for seventeen months, until the Soviets liberated the area in July 1944. While in hiding, Zandman studied mathematics, which helped him become a successful businessman later in life.

The story of Felix Zandman and the Puchalskis is just one example of how ordinary people risked their lives to provide refuge for Jews in Nazi-occupied Europe. Their accounts are as varied as their circumstances, but they all have a common thread: selfless compassion for those who were suffering and desperately in need of help.

Corrie ten Boom's House of Refuge

Compassion for the oppressed was never more fearlessly expressed than by people who hid Jews during the Holocaust. The Netherlands was especially hard-hit by German occupation forces: the Jewish death toll there was the highest of any nation in Western Europe. Swift raids by Dutch policemen and Gestapo (German Secret State Police) agents tore Jews from their homes and sent them to concentration camps. Leaving the country was impossible for Dutch Jews, whose only hope for survival was to go into hiding. For that they needed someone willing to risk his or her life to provide shelter— someone like Cornelia "Corrie" ten Boom.

By the time the Germans occupied the Netherlands in 1940, Corrie ten Boom had lived in "Beje," the house in Haarlem where she grew up, for almost fifty years. As a member of the Dutch Reformed Church, ten Boom had compassion for all people regardless of religion or nationality. The ten Boom family had long championed the cause of improving relations between Christians and Jews. The Nazi occupation of her homeland put ten Boom's faith to the ultimate test.

Welcoming the Unwelcome

One evening in May 1942 a woman carrying a suitcase knocked on the door of Beje. When ten Boom opened the door the woman said, "My name is Kleermaker. I am a Jew."[6] The woman explained that she was afraid to return to her home after a visit from the Gestapo-controlled political police. When she asked for refuge, ten Boom's father answered, "In this household, God's people are always welcome."[7] Two nights later an elderly couple seeking shelter were also taken in. Word spread quickly around Haarlem that Beje had become a refuge for persecuted Jews. "We had not planned our rescue work," ten Boom said later. "People started coming to us stating, 'The Gestapo is behind us,' and we took them in."[8]

> "We had not planned our rescue work. People started coming to us stating, 'The Gestapo is behind us,' and we took them in."[8]
>
> —Corrie ten Boom, Dutch rescuer.

Beje could not hold all the Jews who requested sanctuary. Sending Jews to other safe houses in the Dutch countryside was possible, but only if the refugees had a ration card. These cards were necessary to obtain food, but they were impossible to counterfeit. A family friend named Fred worked at the government office where the cards were distributed, so ten Boom paid him a visit. Fred suggested staging a fake robbery in which cards could be "stolen" and passed on to her. The plan worked. A week later, Fred handed ten Boom one hundred ration cards—safe passage for one hundred Jewish refugees.

The Secret Room

Frequent unannounced raids by the Gestapo or local police collaborators made it dangerous for Dutch citizens to shelter Jews; the next knock on the door could mean a Nazi roundup for the Jews and prison for their hiders. One day the Dutch underground put ten Boom in contact with an architect named Mr. Smit. He offered to build a secret room in Beje to hide Jews during a raid. In ten Boom's third-floor bedroom Smit created a false wall, behind which was a small room that could hide five or six people. In case of a raid, buttons placed strategically around the house could be pressed to trigger a warning buzzer.

The ten Booms held drills to see how quickly refugees could get to the secret room during a raid. Not only people, but every trace of their existence, including clothes, half-eaten food, and even cigar ashes, had to be taken to the room. Eventually the evacuation time was cut to just over one minute. The need for the drills became clear when the Gestapo came to Beje on February 28, 1944.

Raid on Beje

Ten Boom was sick in her bed when the buzzer sounded the alarm. Six people—four Jews and two underground workers—dashed to the third-floor hiding place as Gestapo agents began their search. When the agents reached her bedroom, they pulled her out of bed and asked, "Tell me now, where are you hiding the Jews?" Ten Boom replied, "I don't know what you're talking about."[9] They searched the bedroom, but did not find the entrance to the secret space. Despite being struck several times, ten Boom never revealed the existence of the secret room. The Gestapo left, taking ten Boom and her family and leaving a guard behind. After two days of hiding in the secret room with little

Corrie ten Boom's house in the Netherlands became a refuge for Jews trying to escape the Gestapo. A small hidden room can be seen through a hole cut into the wall; people entered through the bottom shelf of the linen closet.

food and no water, the six refugees managed to escape to freedom with the help of the underground.

Her refugees were free, but ten Boom's ordeal was just beginning. After spending nearly four months in a Dutch prison, she and her sister were sent to the Ravensbrück concentration camp in Germany, where her sister died in December 1944. On January 1, 1945, ten Boom was released and returned to the Netherlands where, after the war, she set up rehabilitation centers for concentration camp survivors. It is estimated that ten Boom saved approximately 800 Dutch Jews from certain death at the hands of the Nazis.

A Savior in Belgium

Belgium, the Netherlands's neighbor to the south, suffered a similar fate under German occupation. When the Germans invaded the Netherlands, Belgium also fell under a vicious air and ground assault

Hiding Anne

Anne Frank is known the world over as the Jewish teenager who, with her family, hid from the Nazis in the Netherlands and recorded her thoughts, feelings, and experiences in a diary. Less well-known is the name of the woman who risked her life to protect the Frank family: Miep Gies.

Gies worked for Anne's father, Otto, in his Amsterdam office. In 1942 Frank told Gies of his plan to hide his family in an annex of the office building, asking for her help in keeping them safe from Nazi raids. Despite deadly consequences if she were discovered helping Jews, Gies agreed. The annex became a secret hiding place for Anne, her parents and sister, and four family friends. While Nazis rounded up Jews on the streets of Amsterdam, Gies shopped for food for the hidden Jews and kept their secret from other office workers.

The family endured nearly two years of living in the annex. Then on August 4, 1944, the Nazis raided the hiding place and the Franks were sent to concentration camps. Only Otto Frank survived the war; Anne died in the Bergen-Belsen concentration camp in February 1945. Gies managed to avoid arrest through the actions of a friendly police officer.

Before the Nazis ransacked the annex, Gies saved a diary that Anne had written during her years in hiding. That book, *The Diary of Anne Frank*, reveals Anne's innermost thoughts during the ordeal of the Holocaust. Without Gies's bravery, it would have been lost forever.

by the Wehrmacht. Once Germany established control of the country, anti-Jewish laws were passed, affecting some seventy thousand Jews. Jewish businesses were shuttered and Jews were forced to wear the yellow Star of David patch. By 1942 Jews were being deported to labor camps in Germany. That same year a priest named Joseph André began saving Belgian Jews.

Born in 1908 André was ordained as a Roman Catholic priest in 1936. A humble and studious but frail man, André was soon posted to the parish of St. Jean-Baptiste in Namur, Belgium. After learning that a Jewish acquaintance, Arthur Burak, faced deportation, André found a place for Burak and his family to hide. The next week two cousins of the Buraks approached André also requesting sanctuary. Again he found a safe haven for the refugees. After these encounters, Father André found he had a new mission: to save Jews being hunted by the Nazis.

Making Contact

In 1942 the Belgian underground established the Jewish Defense Committee (Comité de Défense des Juifs, or CDJ) to find hiding places for Jews. André met with members of the CDJ, offering to find refuge for any Jews, especially children, the organization sent to him. A Jewish activist and CDJ member, identified in records as Mr. Vishnie, describes André helping the group:

> I personally referred many people to Father André, and he always found hiding places for them and arranged their rescue. . . . It was not even necessary to knock on his door, for it was always open. No one ever passed through it without ultimately finding a suitable arrangement. Moreover, he kept tabs on all Jews whom he directed to secure shelters. Convinced that a particular place had become unsuitable or the treatment given was not good enough, he immediately took steps to have the Jews transferred to a new location.[10]

André traveled throughout the region, visiting monasteries and convents as well as private homes in search of places to shelter Jewish children. Many people, moved by André's sincere demeanor, agreed to take in refugee children. Until he could find suitable sanctuaries for his charges, André accommodated children—as many as twenty at a time—in his parish office in Namur. As the center for André's rescue activities, the office was located in a dangerous place: across from the Gestapo *Kommandantur*, or military headquarters. Despite being interrogated several times by the Gestapo, André continued his clandestine rescue efforts without interference.

After Liberation

Eventually, however, the Gestapo began to suspect that André was not the simple priest that he appeared to be. They could not ignore the rumors of Jewish children being spirited to safety by André and his collaborators. Before long he was forced to go into hiding, where he remained until the Allies liberated Namur in September 1944.

Although Belgium had been freed from Nazi tyranny, André's work was not finished. He began reuniting the Jewish children he had sent into hiding with their families. For those children whose parents had been killed by the Nazis, André found charitable organizations willing to take them in. By the fall of 1945 all of André's children were once more with their families or in other accommodations in the community. US Army chaplain Rabbi Harold Saperstein wrote of André in 1945, "He is a gentle, frail fellow—humble in demeanor. . . . Yet he proved himself to be of the stuff of which spiritual heroes are made of."[11] Hundreds of Jewish children owe their lives to this humble priest whose compassion for the oppressed knew no religious boundaries.

> "[Joseph André] is a gentle, frail fellow—humble in demeanor. . . .Yet he proved himself to be of the stuff of which spiritual heroes are made of."[11]
>
> —Rabbi Harold Saperstein.

The Diplomat Rescuer

During the Holocaust, thousands of Jews were kept hidden from the dangers of Nazi occupation by such concerned individuals as Corrie ten Boom and Joseph André. In Budapest, Hungary, thousands more were able to hide in plain sight, protected from Nazi deportation by official-looking documents issued by a brave Swedish diplomat.

Although Hungary was not occupied by German troops until March of 1944, most of its Jewish occupants suffered the same fate as Jews in Poland and other occupied nations. Adolf Eichmann, the Nazi in charge of deporting Jews, commented, "Now the turn of Hungary has come. It will be a deportation surpassing every preceding operation in magnitude."[12] This was no idle threat. More than four hundred thousand Jews from the Hungarian countryside were deported, most facing certain death at Auschwitz. The remaining two hundred thirty thousand Jews lived in the capital city of Budapest. They knew their turn at deportation could come at any moment.

In the United States a War Refugee Board had been established a few months earlier to provide aid to European Jews. When the board learned about the situation in Hungary, it recruited diplomats from neutral countries to help rescue the Jews of Budapest. One of the people asked to join this effort was Raoul Wallenberg of Sweden.

Wallenberg was a businessman who traveled throughout Europe making deals for an import-export company. A shrewd negotiator who was fluent in several languages, Wallenberg seemed to be the perfect man to deal with the situation in Hungary. He agreed to take on this job as long as the Swedish Foreign Ministry met certain conditions, including appointing him to a high diplomatic position. This appointment would allow him to negotiate with whomever he chose. With thousands of Hungarian Jews being murdered at Auschwitz every day, he was impatient to begin his mission. "I can't stay in Sweden until the end of July [as planned]," Wallenberg told his business partner. "Every day costs human lives. I'm going to get ready to leave immediately."[13] On July 9, 1944, carrying a change of clothes, a list of Jews who needed rescue, and a pistol, Wallenberg stepped off a train in Budapest.

Raoul Wallenberg of Sweden (pictured in the 1940s) orchestrated the creation of passports that identified holders as being under Swedish protection. Through his actions, tens of thousands of Hungarian Jews were saved.

Safe Passage

Upon his arrival, Wallenberg established an office inside the Swedish Legation (diplomatic offices) called Section C and recruited a staff to help him. Many of his new colleagues were Jews who held provisional passports that protected them from deportation. These papers gave Wallenberg an idea, as Per Anger, a friend of Wallenberg who worked on his staff, relates in his 1981 memoir:

> The idea of the so-called protective passports was born at our first meeting. These were the identification papers in blue and yellow with the three crowns [the official Swedish crest] on them that would come to be the saving of tens of thousands of Jews.[14]

Called a *Schutzpass*, the new document proclaimed that the bearer was under protection of the Swedish Legation. Since Sweden was a neutral nation, the Nazis considered anyone recognized by the Legation to be safe from persecution. Wallenberg designed the Schutzpass to appear as impressive as possible, knowing that Hungarian bureaucrats would be more receptive to official-looking documents. Although the passes had no legal standing, their appearance made them effective. Initially, fifteen hundred Schutzpasses were printed and distributed; soon the total climbed to forty-five hundred. With more than two hundred thousand Jews at risk, it seemed an overwhelming task—but it was a start.

Swedish Houses

While Section C was processing thousands of Schutzpasses, the political situation of Hungary underwent a drastic upheaval. In October 1944 the government was overthrown by the Arrow Cross, an anti-Semitic (and pro-Nazi) political party. Arrow Cross members began rounding up Jews and shooting them or forcing them on brutal death marches.

Wallenberg had to act quickly. Using money from the War Refugee Board, Wallenberg began to acquire buildings to use as safe houses. He rented thirty-one buildings, each one prominently displaying the Swedish flag to designate the structure as Swedish territory, thus protecting any Jews living there. These Swedish Houses kept some fifteen to twenty thousand Jews from being killed or deported. Joseph Lapid, whose mother had been taken from a safe house, feared

Zegota

After the Nazi occupation of Poland, the nation's leaders established a government in exile, headquartered first in Paris and later in London. Under the auspices of this government, a secret underground organization was formed with the purpose of helping Polish Jews. The Konrad Zegota Committee, commonly known as Zegota, was the code name for the Council to Aid Jews in occupied Poland. Established in October 1942, Zegota was the only organization supported by a government in occupied Europe.

Operating mainly in Warsaw, Zegota was organized into one hundred divisions called cells. Each cell had a specific concentration: medical care, housing, children, clothing, and other areas of need. Zegota operatives provided Jews with food, money, hiding places, and forged identity papers. One notable member of Zegota was Irena Sendler, who helped Jewish children escape from the Warsaw ghetto and worked to reunite them with their families after the war. Zegota also networked with other underground organizations, helping their relief efforts for Polish Jews in other ghettos and concentration camps.

Zegota operated until the liberation of Poland in January 1945. The organization helped save some four thousand Polish Jews and, by working with other organizations, assisted in saving thousands more who would have perished under the Nazi regime.

he would never see her again. But a few hours after her arrest, she returned safely, "It seemed like a mirage, a miracle," Joseph later related. "My mother was there—she was alive and she was hugging and kissing me, and she said one word: 'Wallenberg.'"[15]

In another daring act, Wallenberg drove all night on November 23 to the Hungarian border town of Hegyeshalom where trains carrying Jews were departing for Auschwitz. At the rail station he boldly walked past the guards and began handing out Schutzpasses to as many Jews as he could. When all the passes were distributed, he led the Jews to waiting trucks to return them to safety in Budapest.

Compassion and Courage

As the Soviet Red Army advanced through Hungary in late 1944, Wallenberg was still rescuing Jews and making plans for them in the postwar world. "I'd never be able to go back to Stockholm," he confided to his friend Anger, "without deep down knowing I'd done all anyone could do to save as many Jews as possible."[16] Although he had indeed done all he could, he would never return to Stockholm. Arrested as a German spy by the Soviet secret police on January 17, 1945, Wallenberg was taken to Moscow where he was locked up in the infamous Lubyanka prison. He was never heard from again.

Numerous theories abound concerning Wallenberg's disappearance. At first, the Soviets denied taking him into custody. They later changed their story numerous times, claiming that he had died of a heart attack or in an accident or was executed. Although what really happened to Wallenberg may never be known, his actions in saving tens of thousands of Jews will forever be a part of Holocaust history.

Eight months before World War II ended, the Soviets arrested Raoul Wallenberg on charges of spying for Germany. He was incarcerated at Lubyanka prison and never heard from again.

As thousands of Jews were being sent to certain death in the Holocaust camps, the people around them faced a decision: to help the innocent victims of Nazi oppression or turn away and ignore what was happening in their own towns and villages. Ignoring the situation was the easy, and safe, way to react. That makes it all the more remarkable that so many others chose to risk their lives to help when no one else would. The brave rescuers who provided refuges for Jews are a cross section of humanity, from royalty such as Princess Alice of Greece, who gave refuge to Jews in Athens, to ordinary people like sixteen-year-old Refik Veseli of Albania, who persuaded his parents to shelter a Jewish family. All had one thing in common: compassion for the oppressed and the courage to act on it.

"I'd never be able to go back to Stockholm without deep down knowing I'd done all anyone could do to save as many Jews as possible."[16]

—Raoul Wallenberg, Swedish diplomat.

CHAPTER TWO

Providing a Way Out

In 1938 the situation of the Jews in Europe was rapidly deteriorating. In March, Hitler's army invaded Austria, home to nearly two hundred thousand Jews, and annexed it to the Third Reich. In Germany, Jews were living under the Nuremberg Laws, which placed severe restrictions on Jewish life. In 1933, when Hitler came to power, Jews had begun escaping Germany, emigrating to neighboring countries such as France, Belgium, and the Netherlands. Before the Nazis developed and implemented Hitler's Final Solution, a systematic program of exterminating the Jews, they encouraged Jews to leave the Third Reich.

By 1939 more than three hundred thousand Jews had fled Germany and Austria. But this was only a small fraction of the Jewish population of Europe, which numbered about 9.5 million in 1933. Restrictions on immigration by many nations, including the United States, left the remaining Jews with nowhere to go. When the Nazis officially halted emigration and forced the Jews to move into crowded ghettos, it seemed that escape was impossible. But there was hope, embodied by brave individuals who risked everything to provide a way for thousands of Jews to escape the Nazi death machine.

A French Friar Sees a Need

During World War I, Pierre Péteul, eldest son of a French miller, spent four years as a stretcher bearer on the front lines. In this role, he faced the hazards of enemy fire and the anxiety of life in the trenches. For his bravery under fire he was awarded the prestigious *Croix de Guerre*. In World War II, Péteul again displayed great courage, not in combat, but as a priest rescuing Jews from the Nazis.

Raised a devout Catholic, at age twelve Péteul became attracted to the Capuchins, a religious order of the Roman Catholic Church. He soon left his home to begin religious training in Belgium, where he was an excellent student. His studies were interrupted by World

War I, after which he returned to the religious life. In 1923 he was ordained as a Capuchin friar, taking the name Père (Father) Marie-Benôit. By 1940 he had spent years living and teaching at a monastery in Rome. When the Germans invaded France in May of that year, Benôit returned to his homeland, settling in Marseille in the south of France. There he began his work as a rescuer of Jews.

Jewish Persecution in France

Thousands of Jews fleeing the German advance through Belgium and the Netherlands in 1940 were pouring into France, the southern half of which was governed by the Nazi-collaborationist Vichy government. Anti-Semitic laws placed restrictions on Jews; they could be

Adolf Hitler speaks to thousands of Nazi Storm Troopers in Germany in 1933, the year he came to power. Thousands of Jews immediately sought refuge in other countries but millions more either could not or did not flee.

sent to internment camps or be deported at any time. Troubled by the situation, Benôit vowed to help the Jews. In a postwar interview, Benôit explained how his rescue work started:

> In the beginning at Marseille, I began an action of propaganda when it was still possible to combat antisemitism by means of conferences and study circles as well as family meetings. On several occasions, I visited the [internment] camp of Les Milles to help the administrative internees, to bring their problems to the authorities in Marseille, and to facilitate their departure abroad.[17]

In 1942 Benôit was approached by a woman whose Jewish husband was in a camp near Marseille and in danger of being deported. Benôit agreed to help, stating that the law under which her husband had been arrested was "an immoral one, and one is not allowed to merely ignore such laws but should actively resist them."[18] Using the monastery as his headquarters, Benôit began an operation to help Jews escape from France to neutral countries. As he relates in his memoirs, Benôit and his volunteer staff would "provide them with identity cards under different names . . . [and] hide them temporarily . . . while they waited to escape to Spain or Switzerland."[19] He traveled throughout France contacting the French underground as well as Jewish and Christian organizations to help with transporting Jews to safety.

An Audience with the Pope

In 1943 Benôit's travels took him to Rome with a new plan to present to Pope Pius XII. The French borders with Spain and Switzerland were closed, leaving the fate of some thirty thousand Jews in Nice, France, uncertain. Benôit's plan was to relocate these Jewish refugees to Italy and then to Allied-held North Africa, but he needed the pope to use his considerable influence on the Italian government to gain its approval. On July 16 Benôit presented his idea to Pope Pius XII, who took the matter under advisement. But the changing tides of war thwarted Benôit's plan when German forces invaded Italy in anticipation of an Italian/Allied cease-fire, eliminating any chance of transferring the Jews.

The Evian Conference

The resort town of Evian-les-Bains in southeastern France has long been famous for its mineral springs, which many people believe have healing powers. There, in July 1938, President Franklin D. Roosevelt assembled an international group of government and private-sector leaders to discuss the problem of relief for the increasing number of Jews fleeing Nazi-occupied Europe.

For nine days delegates from thirty-two nations and thirty-nine relief organizations met in the luxurious Hôtel Royal near Lake Geneva. The outcome of the conference had been decided in advance, because Roosevelt had assured delegates that they would not be forced to increase their current immigration quotas. One by one the delegates expressed their sympathy for the oppressed Jews and condemned the Nazis for their anti-Semitic practices. But none offered to help alleviate the situation. Illustrating the tone of the conference was a comment made by the Australian delegate T.W. White: "It will no doubt be appreciated," he said, "that as we have no racial problem, we are not desirous of importing one." In the end, only the tiny Caribbean island nation of the Dominican Republic offered to take in a substantial number of Jews—up to 100,000 refugees.

The Evian Conference represented a major disappointment for the world's Jews and a propaganda gold mine for Adolf Hitler. He gloated over the fact that so many countries had criticized Germany's treatment of the Jews and had professed great sympathy for their plight, yet none of these countries wanted to allow them entry when the opportunity arose.

Quoted in Martin Gilbert, *The Holocaust: A History of the Jews of Europe During the Second World War.* New York: Holt, Rinehart and Winston, 1985, p. 64.

Although disappointed by the failure of his Italian plan, Benôit continued his activities in support of the Jews. After a meeting with some newly arrived refugees, he wrote, "It was impossible for me not to resume the duties of my assistance work."[20] He made Rome his new base of operations and contacted the Delegation for the Assistance of Jewish Emigrants (Delasem), an Italian aid organization funneling money to Jewish refugees. For nine months Benôit worked with Delasem, creating false identity papers and providing temporary shelter, resulting in the rescue of thousands of Jews. Benôit's actions soon came to the attention of the Gestapo, and he was forced to go into hiding. He was still working to help the Jews when Allied forces liberated Rome in June 1944. Although exact numbers do not exist, Benôit unquestionably helped save thousands of Jews from being deported to the Nazi camps. "What I did for the Jewish people," Benôit wrote in 1978, "what I did to merit being called 'Father of the Jews' is but an infinitesimal contribution of what should have been done to prevent this most heinous and satanic slaughter of some six million Jews."[21] The friar's humble words belie the extraordinary nature of his actions and the courage required to carry them out.

> "What I did for the Jewish people, what I did to merit being called 'Father of the Jews' is but an infinitesimal contribution of what should have been done to prevent this most heinous and satanic slaughter of some six million Jews."[21]
>
> —Père Marie-Benôit, Capuchin friar.

The Defiant Consul

Père Marie-Benôit saved thousands of Jews by obeying his religious belief in the equality of all people. Sometimes, however, doing the right thing requires disobedience to those who are in positions of power. During the Holocaust countless Jewish lives were saved by people defying the law and going against authority regardless of the consequences. One such rescuer was Aristides de Sousa Mendes, a Portuguese consul stationed in the city of Bordeaux in southwestern France.

Mendes, a career diplomat, had worked in consulates all over the world when he was posted as Portuguese consul general to Bordeaux in 1938. When Hitler's armies began spreading across Europe, neutral Portugal became a gateway for persecuted people to escape to freedom. Then Germany invaded Poland in September 1939 and the flood of refugees increased by thousands. Fearing the influx of immigrants would undermine his regime, Portuguese president Antonio de Oliveira Salazar tightened the borders of his nation to those fleeing the Nazi menace—especially Jews.

Fearing an influx of fleeing Jews, Portuguese president Antonio de Oliveira Salazar (pictured) ordered his country's borders closed to Jews in 1939. Aristides de Sousa Mendes, a Portuguese consul stationed in France, defied Salazar's orders by issuing and distributing thousands of travel visas to Jews.

On November 11, 1939, Salazar issued a directive to all of his consuls. Known as Circular 14, it forbid the consuls from allowing refugees, especially "Jews expelled from the countries of their nationality,"[22] to claim safe haven in Portugal without approval of the Foreign Minister (a post also held by Salazar). In Bordeaux, Mendes, who was already issuing visas in certain cases, ignored the directive despite the consequences of disobeying his superior. After France fell to the Germans, Mendes was reminded once more to stop distributing visas. But his conscience would not let him quit.

Refugees soon flooded Bordeaux, camping out on the streets and surrounding the consulate where Mendes worked and begging for the coveted visas. One night Mendes met Polish rabbi Chaim Kruger, an encounter that changed everything for the consul general. Mendes

Finding Refuge in Asia

In Nazi-occupied Europe, most Jews who sought to escape the horrors of the Holocaust did so by traveling to neutral European nations such as Switzerland and Portugal. Some refugees, however, looked toward Asia to find a safe haven. One destination was the Chinese port city of Shanghai.

China in the late 1930s was locked in a vicious war with Japan. The wartime chaos in the country had made a shambles of passport regulations; anyone could enter the country without official papers. Thousands of European Jews took advantage of the situation and made the monthlong voyage to freedom, a journey that ended at the docks in Shanghai. Although there was safety for the Jews in Shanghai, life was difficult. Forced to live in a run-down slum, a ghetto reminiscent of the Jewish ghettos in Europe, the Jewish refugees struggled to survive. Food and money were scarce, and jobs almost impossible to find. Most Jews in Shanghai subsisted on charity provided by American and Jewish relief agencies.

With the onset of World War II in 1939, the tide of Jewish refugees to China was halted. Between 1937 and 1941 about twenty thousand Jews found refuge in Shanghai. After the war they left Asia to start new lives in the United States, Canada, and Australia.

offered to issue a visa for him and his family. Kruger's response was to challenge Mendes: "I thanked him for his generosity . . . and explained that there was only one avenue of escape—to give all of us visas to Portugal."[23] Mendes went into seclusion to consider the implications of the rabbi's request. After several anguished nights, he reached a decision: "From now on I'm giving everyone visas. There will be no more nationalities, races, or religions."[24]

Mendes immediately began an assembly-line operation that turned out visas as quickly as the official marks could be stamped on passports. Volunteers, including Rabbi Kruger, helped keep the operation rolling. When a staff member implored him to stop this illegal activity, Mendes told his workers, "My government has denied all applications for visas to any refugees. But I cannot allow these people to die."[25]

Dire Consequences

In the space of several days, Mendes was able to issue some thirty thousand visas; about twelve thousand of those were distributed to Jews. The visas were honored at the border between Spain and Portugal, allowing their bearers to enter the country. The Jews were safe, but Mendes's insubordination to the Portuguese authorities triggered his downfall. He was summoned back to Lisbon, Portugal's capital city, where he was forced to retire from his official position and denied the retirement benefits he had accrued during his long diplomatic career. After his dismissal, Mendes told Rabbi Kruger, "I could not have acted otherwise, and I therefore accept all that has befallen me with love."[26]

With no chance of further employment, Mendes sold his home to pay off debts and buy food for his children. Fittingly, his family received some assistance from the Hebrew Immigrant Aid Society, a Jewish charity. When Mendes died at age 68 in 1954, he was a destitute and forgotten man. But his deeds will be remembered, especially by the descendants of the thirty thousand people he saved. According to historian Yehuda Bauer, Mendes accomplished "perhaps the largest rescue action by a single individual during the Holocaust."[27]

> "From now on I'm giving everyone visas. There will be no more nationalities, races, or religions."[24]
>
> —Aristides de Sousa Mendes, Portuguese consul.

Winton's Children

Even before the German occupation of France, Czechoslovakia in Eastern Europe had been subjected to the tyranny of Hitler's Third Reich. In October 1938 Germany annexed the Sudetenland, several strips of Czech territory along the German border. Many ethnic Germans lived within that region, as did thousands of Jews. As German troops paraded through the streets, Jews began fleeing eastward to the Czech capital of Prague. Without any available shelter, they set up makeshift refugee camps. It was the sight of these camps that inspired a British stockbroker to help the beleaguered Jews.

Nicholas Winton was at home in London preparing for his annual Christmas ski trip to Switzerland when a phone call from a friend named Martin Blake caused him to change his plans. Blake persuaded Winton to come to Prague where he was working to aid Jewish refugees. What Winton saw in December 1938 in the Czech capital greatly affected him.

> The situation was heartbreaking. Many of the refugees hadn't the price of a meal. Some of the mothers tried desperately to get money to buy food for themselves and their children. The parents desperately wanted at least to get their children to safety when they couldn't manage to get visas for the whole family. I began to realize what suffering there is when armies start to march.[28]

Winton searched without success for groups that were helping the children. "Everybody in Prague said 'Look, there is no organization in Prague to deal with refugee children, nobody will let the children go on their own, but if you want to have a go, have a go.'"[29] That was all Winton needed to begin his own rescue operation.

Rescue by Rail

Winton's hotel room in Prague became his headquarters. He contacted representatives of numerous countries to find a refuge for the children; only the governments of England and Sweden offered to help. He immediately began signing children up for their journey to freedom. As word spread of Winton's activities, hundreds of anxious parents lined up at the hotel, hoping that their children would be chosen. The British Home Office, the department responsible for immigration, required that each child have a place to stay upon leaving Czechoslovakia and a £50 (about $200 at the time) guarantee to pay for the passage.

"The situation [in Prague] was heartbreaking. Many of the refugees hadn't the price of a meal. Some of the mothers tried desperately to get money to buy food for themselves and their children. . . . I began to realize what suffering there is when armies start to march."[28]

—Nicholas Winton, British businessman.

Briton Nicholas Winton receives an award from the president of the Czech Republic in 2014. Winton orchestrated a program that brought hundreds of Jewish children from Czechoslovakia to safety in Britain in 1939.

Winton's working vacation in Czechoslovakia was soon over. He returned to London to line up families to take in the Jewish refugee children, while volunteers continued to register more children. Working at night after a full day at the stock exchange, Winton raised money for the guarantees and located foster families as required by the Home Office. Most of the rescues started off by rail. The first trainload of children left Prague on March 14, 1939, on a route that took them through Czechoslovakia, Nazi Germany, and finally the Netherlands. The children then boarded a ferry for the last leg of the journey to safety in England. This effort was similar to the *Kindertransport*, which brought young German and Austrian Jews to England around the same time. Winton's operation did the same for the children of Czechoslovakia. Between late March and August 2, seven more trains traveled along the same rescue route. A total of 669 children were safely transported to sponsoring families in England. However, Winton's efforts were about to come to an abrupt end.

The Ninth Train

A ninth refugee train was scheduled to leave Prague on September 3, 1939. It would be the largest rescue yet, with some 250 children waiting to travel to safety in England. On September 1, however, German troops invaded Poland and all German borders were closed; Winton's escape route vanished. The fate of those 250 children haunted Winton for the rest of his life.

> Within hours of the announcement [of the invasion], the train disappeared. None of the 250 children aboard was seen again. We had 250 families waiting at Liverpool Street that day in vain. If the train had been a day earlier, it would have come through. Not a single one of those children was heard of again, which is an awful feeling.[30]

Echoing the sentiments of most Holocaust rescuers, Winton never wished to be viewed as a hero. "It turned out to be remarkable," he later recalled, "but it didn't seem remarkable when I did it."[31] In fact, he remained silent about his rescue operation for fifty years, until a scrapbook with the names of rescued children was discovered by his wife. Reunions of "Winton's Children," as they called themselves, afforded them the opportunity to reminisce and to honor the man who saved them. It is estimated that more than five thousand people owe their lives to Winton as descendants of the original Winton's Children.

A Strong Moral Compass

The Holocaust was a time when evil seemed strong enough to overpower good. "In this mad world," psychologist Eva Fogelman explains, "most people lost their bearings. Fear disoriented them, and self-protection blinded them. A few, however, did not lose their way. A few took their direction from their own moral compass."[32] Among those few were the brave individuals who helped the Jews escape the Nazi menace.

CHAPTER THREE

Aid and Rescue Groups

France in 1940 was a divided nation under siege. Hitler's army had invaded France on May 10, and troops quickly advanced through the countryside, eventually occupying the northern half of the country. The southern portion remained temporarily unoccupied and administered by the Vichy government, outwardly free but in reality a puppet regime subservient to German authority. As in Germany, anti-Semitic laws were passed curtailing the rights of Jews, barring them from many occupations and requiring the confiscation of such valuable items as radios, bicycles, and telephones. In 1942 the Nazis began deporting Jews to extermination camps in Eastern Europe.

Even before the beginning of World War II, numerous social welfare agencies around the world were helping oppressed Jews. Many had provided food, shelter, and hope to European Jews since before the First World War. With the onset of this new global conflict, Jewish relief societies faced their greatest challenge. They provided financial support, arranged for temporary shelters, and assisted Jews in imminent threat of deportation to relocate to safe havens abroad.

In addition to formal organizations, ordinary people often banded together at great personal risk to help their fellow souls in need. Active throughout the war, these included religious groups, youth organizations, underground units, and even entire towns. Whether permanent organizations or temporary alliances, working openly or in secret, these groups were ultimately responsible for saving thousands of Jewish lives.

To Save the Children

Rescuing children became a major objective for Jewish social-welfare agencies during the Holocaust. Jews had been living under increasing oppression since the rise of the Nazis in the early 1930s. Then came

Kristallnacht ("Night of Broken Glass") in November 1938, when Nazi troops rampaged through Jewish neighborhoods, destroying businesses and murdering Jews in the streets. In these desperate circumstances, the Jews began looking for ways to save their children even if they could not save themselves. One organization dedicated to aiding children in need was the French-Jewish organization Oeuvre de Secours aux Enfants (OSE), or Children's Relief Agency.

The OSE was established in 1912 by doctors in St. Petersburg, Russia, as a health care organization for needy Russian Jews. In 1933 the OSE relocated its headquarters to Paris, and by 1938 the organization was specializing in the care of Jewish children, creating a series of homes, or châteaux, for refugee children. One such house in Montmorency, the Villa Helvetia, became a shelter for more than three

Several organizations launched programs to save Jewish children from the Nazis after the violent 1938 anti-Jewish riots known as Kristallnacht. The smashed windows of a printing company owned by Jews can be seen in this photo taken in Berlin shortly after the riots.

hundred Jewish children. Eventually more châteaux were established, ultimately numbering eleven homes caring for sixteen hundred children whose parents had been deported to concentration camps. Most of these children would never see their parents again.

French Internment Camps

In addition to sheltering Jewish youth, the OSE helped many children escape from the Nazi menace. With German backing, the Vichy government administered numerous internment camps in southern France including Gurs, located fifty miles (80.4 km) from France's border with Spain. Beginning in 1940 between seventeen thousand and twenty-two thousand Jewish men, women, and children were interned at Gurs. Several hundred miles to the east another camp, Rivesaltes, held Jews, Roma (Gypsies), and other people the Third Reich considered either "undesirables" or enemies. At Gurs children were separated from their families; at Rivesaltes children were allowed to stay with their parents. Living conditions behind the barbed-wire fences of both camps were harsh; thousands died due to disease and starvation. Soon Vichy officials began relocating Jews to the Drancy transit camp in the north, where they were eventually transported to Auschwitz.

Rescuing children from the camps became a priority for the OSE. Working with French authorities, the organization obtained permission to remove children from Gurs and Rivesaltes if it could prove the children had a place to stay. This usually meant that rescued children stayed at one of the OSE châteaux until other arrangements could be made. Although the children's welfare naturally came first, it was difficult for the parents to let them go. One such separation is described by Vivette Samuel, an OSE social worker:

> The parents had been granted the favor of accompanying their children to the trucks. . . . Parents and children were then separated. No one cried, as the last recommendations were given and bags were checked. After the last call the camp gates were opened. . . . The children sang heartily in the wind and the cold and the dark to show the joy of being free again. And the parents' tears began to flow. Would they ever see their children again?[33]

Mossad le-Aliyah Bet

Since ancient times, Palestine has been home to numerous peoples: Greeks, Persians, Babylonians, Assyrians, Arabs, and Jews. Between 1920 and 1948 the region was a British Mandate, controlled by Great Britain. In 1938, as thousands of Jews fled the Third Reich, the British began restricting Jewish admission to Palestine. The next year Mossad le-Aliyah Bet was formed.

In Hebrew, "Aliyah Aleph" meant Immigration A, or legal immigration; "Aliyah Bet," (Immigration B) signified a second kind of immigration—illegal. Mossad le-Aliyah Bet (Organization for Illegal Immigration) coordinated the efforts of Jews seeking to immigrate to Palestine. It was not an easy process: funds were scarce, the voyages were dangerous, and the British had set up a blockade of Palestine. Aliyah Bet ships could be sunk by German U-boats or captured and turned back by British blockade ships. Such conditions led to the temporary halting of resettlement operations, which did not resume until 1944. Despite the hardships, between 1937 and 1944 more than sixty voyages under the auspices of Mossad le-Aliyah Bet safely relocated thousands of Jews to Palestine.

Mossad le-Aliyah Bet continued its resettlement operations after the war, although it continued to face British opposition. By 1948, when the State of Israel was established in Palestine, Mossad le-Aliyah Bet had enabled more than one hundred thousand Jewish refugees to begin a new life in an ancient land.

At the OSE houses, the children were fed nutritious meals to make up for the months of near-starvation rations provided at the camps. Many eventually boarded ships and made their way to the United States. By June 1942 more than six hundred children had been rescued from the camps with the help of the OSE. By the time France was liberated in 1944, about forty-six hundred Jewish children were being cared for by the OSE.

Funding Rescue

Humanitarian groups such as the OSE could not have operated as efficiently as they did without receiving support from agencies sympathetic to their causes. One such organization was headquartered in the United States, but its outreach was worldwide. Since its beginning in 1914 the American Jewish Joint Distribution Committee (JDC) provided assistance for Jewish refugees around the world. After World War I the JDC helped Jews in Poland and Russia who were left destitute by the war.

The German occupation of France and the subsequent deportation of Jews to the East raised an alarm within the JDC, especially in regard to Jewish children. Joseph C. Hyman, executive vice-chairman of the JDC in 1942, describes the situation in France at the time.

> "Thousands of Jewish mothers in Paris, given the choice of keeping their children with them or leaving them behind, preferred to part from their infants rather than take them along to unknown destinations."[34]
>
> —Joseph C. Hyman, executive vice-chairman of the JDC.

The recent deportation to eastern Poland and occupied Russia of 12,000 Jews from Paris and other parts of occupied France has aroused terror in the hearts of the entire Jewish population. Thousands of Jewish mothers in Paris, given the choice of keeping their children with them or leaving them behind, preferred to part from their infants rather than take them along to unknown destinations. It is these children, orphaned for at least the duration of the war, who will be brought to homes of safety in southern France where they can receive adequate care.[34]

The JDC contributed $25,000 to support the rescue of some twelve hundred children from northern France. Other agencies depended on the JDC for desperately needed funds for refugees in neutral nations such as Spain and Switzerland. "Many hundreds of desperate people," Hyman continued, "have fled across the borders of France, especially into Switzerland, during recent weeks. They need assistance of every kind and it is the Joint Distribution Committee which is looked to for the financial help necessary."[35]

The JDC funded rescue operations in more than forty nations, some as far away as China. Poland, for example, received aid to provide temporary shelter, food, and medical care for some six hundred thousand Jewish refugees in 1940. The urgent need for Jews to emigrate from occupied Europe prompted the JDC to fund operations that helped send refugees to safety in the United States, Latin America, and Palestine.

The Voyage of the *St. Louis*

Not all rescue missions supported by the JDC succeeded. On May 13, 1939, the passenger ship *St. Louis* left Hamburg, Germany, carrying 937 Jewish refugees. The ship headed for Cuba, where it was to await permission to enter the United States. When the ship reached Havana, however, the passengers discovered that Cuban immigration policy had changed and they would not be allowed to disembark. The next day a JDC representative arrived in Cuba to negotiate with President Federico Bru on behalf of the refugees. But Bru was not persuaded and ordered the *St. Louis* to leave Cuba. As the ship sailed north along the coast of Florida, the refugees hoped to be allowed to enter the United States directly. But they were turned away.

The return voyage for the Jews was one of disappointment and fear of what waited for them back in Europe. "This is one of the most tragic days on board," wrote passenger Josef Joseph in his diary, "because we feel cheated for the freedom we had hoped for. What started as a voyage of freedom is now a voyage of doom."[36]

Not giving up, the JDC contacted several nations in hopes of finding places for the refugees. By the time the *St. Louis* returned to Europe on June 17, shelters for the refugees had been secured in England, the Netherlands, Belgium, and France. No one could foresee that only the refugees going to England would be safe. The other three nations ultimately fell to the Nazi advance. Two hundred fifty-four passengers of the *St. Louis* perished in Holocaust camps and killing centers.

Forced to operate clandestinely in Europe after the invasion of France in 1940, the JDC nevertheless continued funding Jewish relief

Jewish refugees from Germany arrive in Belgium in 1939 aboard the St. Louis. After being denied entry to Cuba and the United States, the ship was forced to return to Europe.

efforts. By 1944 more than eighty thousand Jewish refugees were living safely outside occupied Europe, due in no small part to $70 million raised by the JDC. For Jewish Americans who lived far from the Nazi menace, the JDC was the principal means of helping fellow Jews caught in a web of terror and destruction.

Faith and Rescue

Among the many organizations the JDC had worked with in the past was the Religious Society of Friends, also known as the Quakers. During World War I, the JDC had contributed financially to the Quaker assistance program for victims of that conflict. In the years leading up to World War II, the Quakers again responded to people in need; they became one of the most active rescue groups during the Holocaust.

Known for their belief in the equality of all people and a commitment to nonviolence, Quakers view humanitarian work an essential part of their faith. American Quakers carried out this work through the American Friends Service Committee (AFSC), an organization dedicated to advancing social justice worldwide. The Friends Ambulance Unit had provided relief for air raid victims during the Blitz, the 1940 German bombing of London. The AFSC also helped Jews escape from Germany and created shelters for refugees in occupied France.

> "The Quakers were trustworthy. Their readiness to help, and help even people who were not actually their friends, left a great impression and smoothed paths—even with the Nazis."[39]
>
> —Franz von Hammerstein, Protestant minister.

At first the Nazis allowed German Quakers to continue the humanitarian work they had begun during World War I. Following Kristallnacht, the international Quaker office in Berlin was inundated with Jews seeking escape. "After that," remembers Quaker Gisela Faust, who was thirteen years old when she witnessed the scene in Berlin, "people stood in line in front of the Quaker office near the Friedrichstrasse station, because everyone realized that the only hope was to try to emigrate at the last minute."[37] When emigration became impossible, Quakers gave food and medical care to Jews interned in camps and ghettos.

Quakers also provided relief services in southern France, which was controlled by a German puppet government. This included feeding some fifty thousand children in the span of about five months and negotiating the issuance of visas for Jews to travel to safe nations. Still, many rescue activities had to be done covertly so as not to jeopardize their ongoing relief mission. Alice Resch, a Quaker volunteer, describes in her memoirs her rescue work in southern France:

From that time [1942] until the liberation, we worked almost daily, hiding both adults and children and securing false identity papers and ration cards. But all this was done on the sly, even among us in the office. We were a neutral, non-political organization after all, and foreigners to boot. We had to be very, very careful not to compromise our work in the camps and for the French children.[38]

Quakers in Britain

Members of the Society of Friends in Great Britain also played an important role in saving thousands of Jews from the Holocaust. British Quakers secured a monetary guarantee of £350,000 ($1.4 million), payable to the British government for the immigration of about six thousand Jewish refugees. Once in the country, the refugees were given shelter and jobs by local Quaker meetings, or congregations. British Quakers also played a leading role in the Kindertransport, a massive operation in 1938 and 1939 that evacuated some ten thousand children by rail and boat from occupied territories to safety in England.

A memorial to those who took part in a series of rescue efforts that brought thousands of Jewish children to Britain from Nazi Germany stands today in the German capital of Berlin. That effort is known as the Kindertransport.

One Thousand Children

In 1938 and 1939 the rescue operation known as the Kindertransport carried ten thousand children to safety in England. But there was another group of rescued Jewish children whose story is lesser known and little remembered. They are the One Thousand Children.

Restricted to 1.5 percent of the school population and shunned by formerly friendly schoolmates, Jewish children in Germany suffered as much under Nazi rule as did the adults. Many Jewish parents, unable to escape the growing Nazi menace, sought ways to save their children. Between 1934 and 1945 more than one thousand Jewish children, ranging from fourteen months to sixteen years of age, were transported to the United States with the help of numerous humanitarian agencies. The American Jewish Joint Distribution Committee (JDC), Oeuvres de Secours aux Enfants (OSE), the Quakers, and many other organizations and individuals worked to secure visas for the children. They operated quietly and without publicity, mindful of American anti-Semitism that could shut them down at any moment.

The children were separated from their families for their voyage to freedom; most would never see their parents again. Once in the United States they were placed with foster families or lived in group homes. Being alone in a new country and living with strangers, as well as worrying about their parents' uncertain fate, took an emotional toll on the children. Many, however, grew up to become teachers, scientists, diplomats, and other productive members of society.

The reason the Quakers could accomplish so much good during the Holocaust was expressed by Franz von Hammerstein, a Protestant minister. "The Quakers were trustworthy. Their readiness to help, and help even people who were not actually their friends, left a great impression and smoothed paths—even with the Nazis."[39]

Rescue in Denmark

People were the heart of Jewish rescue operations, whether individually or in organized and funded groups. Sometimes individuals banded together to accomplish a goal when circumstances presented an opportunity for helping others. In several countries citizens rallied to provide assistance to persecuted Jews when there was no other means of help.

When the Nazis overran Denmark in April 1940, officials promised to cooperate with the Germans; they anticipated that Denmark would become a model protectorate of the Third Reich. The Nazis were at first tolerant of the nation's nearly eight thousand Jews who had integrated into Danish society. Unlike such occupied nations as Poland, France, and Czechoslovakia, Denmark had no ghettos or concentration camps. But continued activities of the Danish underground caused the Nazis to eventually crack down on the Danish Jews. In 1943 a mass roundup was planned to send every Jew in Denmark to concentration camps.

News of the Nazi plan set the nation into action. Hans Fuglsang Damgaard, bishop of Copenhagen, wrote a stirring pastoral letter in which he said, "We will fight for our Jewish brothers and sisters to be able to retain the same liberty that we ourselves esteem higher than life itself."[40] That liberty came in the form of boats of all sizes and types, piloted by fishermen and other captains who ferried Jews across the narrow strait that separates Denmark from neutral Sweden. Countless Danish citizens risked their lives to shelter the Jews until spaces on the boats could be found.

> "We will fight for our Jewish brothers and sisters to be able to retain the same liberty that we ourselves esteem higher than life itself."[40]
>
> —Hans Fuglsang Damgaard, bishop of Copenhagen.

When the Nazis conducted their roundup on October 1, only a few hundred Jews were found. Thanks to the citizens of Denmark, more than seven thousand Danish Jews had been whisked to safely in Sweden.

The Town That Cared

After Hitler's army occupied northern France, finding places of refuge became vital to the survival of French Jews. Thousands fled south to the unoccupied Vichy region, looking for people to take them in. One town located high on a plateau became a leader in providing shelter for Jewish children. Le Chambon-sur-Lignon was a village of farmers descended from a once-oppressed Christian sect called Huguenots. The knowledge that their ancestors had once been outcasts gave the people of Le Chambon an understanding of what the refugee Jews were going through. So they decided to help.

André Trocmé, pastor of the Protestant church in Le Chambon, urged his congregation to open their homes despite the danger that hiding Jews presented. In a 1990 interview Nelly Trocmé Hewett, the pastor's daughter, explained her father's leadership:

> My father was not the one who really sheltered them, although we had four Jewish people in our own house. But he was one of the people, one of the leaders of the community, who inspired the population and kept giving the people courage and kept putting them in front of their duty, to give them the strength it took really to do that kind of thing.[41]

Throughout Le Chambon and the other villages on the plateau, people opened their homes to Jewish children who had been sent by parents who could not leave occupied territories themselves. During the early 1940s trainloads of children arrived daily on the plateau. In individual or group homes, the children were fed, educated, and kept safe from the probing of Nazi patrols that occasionally swept the villages. By the time France was liberated in 1944, some three thousand to five thousand lives had been saved by the people of Le Chambon and the surrounding villages.

In times of disaster, people tend to come together to help, console one another, or simply be there for each other. For the Jews of Europe, no time was more disastrous than the Holocaust. The groups of humanitarians, religious leaders, and ordinary people who risked their lives so others could escape the Nazi menace provided a bright example of the goodness of humanity in a world of darkness.

CHAPTER FOUR

Liberation from the East

By early 1942 Hitler's Wehrmacht (armed forces) seemed invincible. After annexing Austria in 1938 and conquering Czechoslovakia in 1939, lightning strikes by German troops, tanks, and aircraft brought most of the rest of Europe into the Third Reich. His one failure, the conquest of England, caused Hitler to look toward the Soviet Union for another nation to defeat. Despite a nonaggression pact signed between the two nations in 1939, Hitler moved forward with his plans to invade the Soviet Union. It was a mistake that would ultimately cost Germany the war.

The invasion began on June 22, 1941. At first the ill-prepared Soviet Red Army was no match for Hitler's battle-hardened troops. But the brutal Russian winter and Germany's failure to capture the Soviet capital of Moscow turned what Hitler had envisioned as a quick victory into a bloody, four-year-long struggle. By early 1944 the Red Army began pushing German troops out of the Soviet territory they had gained. In July the Soviets defeated one of Germany's main forces and advanced into occupied Poland. As Soviet tanks and troops approached the town of Lublin on July 23, they discovered one of the Nazis' most brutal extermination camps.

Liberating Majdanek

Majdanek is located about two miles (3.2 km) outside of the town of Lublin. Built as a concentration camp for Russian prisoners of war in 1941, Majdanek later became both a labor camp and killing center. Jews, as well as non-Jewish Poles, were brought to Majdanek from the surrounding area and from other camps that had been closed by the Nazis. Ultimately people from some thirty countries were imprisoned at Majdanek. The prisoners were put to work as slave laborers, performing backbreaking work until they died of exhaustion, malnutrition, or disease. Those who survived the hard labor or were too weak to work were killed in the camp's three gas chambers, their bodies burned in the crematorium. Exact numbers are difficult to determine, but it is estimated that about eighty thousand prisoners, two-thirds of which were Jews, died at Majdanek.

Although Nazi camps had been in existence for years, few people besides the Nazi hierarchy and the prisoners themselves knew what really went on there. Rumors had circulated about mass killings of Jews, but the stories were dismissed as far-fetched tales that could not possibly be true. When troops of the Soviet Second Tank Army entered Majdanek, they were unprepared for what they found. "When we saw what it contained," commented a political commissar traveling with the troops, "we felt dangerously close to going insane."[42] Historian Joshua Rubenstein describes the scene before them:

> "There was a whole warehouse full of shoes, hundreds of thousands of them, piled high to the ceiling, in all sorts of sizes. Many of them were children's. Our soldiers asked each other in bewilderment: 'What has been going on here?'"[44]
>
> —Soviet captain Anatoly Mereshko.

Initially, the soldiers did not understand what they were finding. They had not been ordered to capture this particular site for any particular reason. But seeing the high walls and the large gate, they figured it was a sufficiently important enterprise to warrant inspection. The brick buildings, the smoke-stacks, the barracks—they all signified some kind of factory or industrial plant. But as the soldiers opened the doors to a gas chamber, an officer explained to them what they were about to see and how it operated. Not long after, they came across a crematorium that was still warm.[43]

Inside the camp unburied corpses lay in stacks along with piles of bones and skulls bleaching in the sun. The Soviet soldiers walked silently past rows of barracks into the gas chambers, the cremato-rium, and storehouses of victims' personal belongings. "There was a whole warehouse full of shoes," commented Soviet captain Anatoly Mereshko, "hundreds of thousands of them, piled high to the ceiling, in all sorts of sizes. Many of them were children's. Our soldiers asked each other in bewilderment: 'What has been going on here?'"[44] A count later revealed that there were eight hundred thousand shoes in the warehouse.

Members of the German armed forces attack a Russian bunker with a flamethrower in 1941. Hitler's vision of a quick victory against the Soviets turned into a bloody, four-year-long struggle that contributed to the German defeat and the liberation of Holocaust camps.

The Difficulty of Belief

When Soviet news reports began to appear after the liberation of Majdanek, it became clear that the films, photographs, and descriptions of the camp were almost too horrible to accept as true. Historian David Shneer describes the problem of believing the unbelievable:

> When Majdanek was liberated the concept of a facility designed for industrial murder using a cyanide-based pesticide was completely foreign, so Soviet journalists reported extensively on everything that made Majdanek so terrifyingly unique. . . . Reports of a death camp in Lublin cropped up sporadically in the western media shortly after the Soviet press broke the news. But the photographs languished while editors and government officials stared dumbly, unsure of what to do with the shocking material. Western officials and media often dismissed Soviet press reports about German atrocities as propaganda, and many newspaper editors found the descriptions of Majdanek too monstrous to believe. . . . It was not until late August [1944] that Soviet occupation forces opened the camp to Lublin's residents and western journalists. If Soviet photographs were not convincing, perhaps eyewitness accounts would be.

Quoted in David Shneer, "Soviet Soldiers Found the First Proof of Germany's Murder Machine. Nobody Believed Them," *World War II*, July/August 2013, pp. 53, 54, 56.

The Survivors of Majdanek

The evidence of the people killed at Majdanek was a gruesome discovery for the Soviet soldiers. But even more unsettling was their encounter with those who had managed to survive the Nazi atrocities. In early 1944 the Germans knew that the Red Army would eventually overrun Majdanek. They realized that any prisoners left alive could provide eyewitness testimony about the atrocities that took place at the camp. In addition, slave workers were still needed in labor camps to continue producing war materiels for the beleaguered Wehrmacht. In March the camp guards began evacuating inmates, and by April some fifteen thousand prisoners had been relocated to Mauthausen, Auschwitz, Ravensbrück, and other camps in the west.

As the Red Army approached Majdanek in July, the Nazis destroyed incriminating camp documents. They attempted to burn down the crematorium but only managed to destroy the wooden structure that surrounded the ovens. A day before the Soviets discovered the camp, guards led some one thousand of the remaining prisoners on a march toward the west. That left about one thousand prisoners in the camp when the Soviets arrived. Many of the survivors were Soviet prisoners of war who bore wounds, missing limbs, or other scars of battle. Other prisoners, both men and women, were so emaciated and ravaged by disease that they were described by a Russian journalist as "living corpses."[45] Medical assistance for these survivors became a priority, but many of them, especially those in psychological distress, were beyond help. Soviet Army nurse Anisya Zenkova describes the situation in the wake of liberation:

> We set up a hospital to treat the inmates from the camp. . . . We tried to help them. Many had TB; others were suffering from deep psychological trauma. It was very hard to reach them, to re-establish a human connection. There was no longer the will to live. These patients would often predict their own death, although there was nothing physically wrong with them, simply announcing: "I will die tomorrow." And that is what invariably happened. We had six or seven such deaths every day.[46]

Revealing the Evidence

The Soviet troops who liberated Majdanek saw firsthand the gruesome evidence of Hitler's Final Solution. Soon after the soldiers liberated the camp, it was the world's turn to learn about Nazi atrocities. Russian journalists, filmmakers, and photographers were allowed to visit Majdanek to document the horrors uncovered by the Red Army. Soviet war correspondent Konstantin Simonov wrote the first published report about Majdanek, entitled "The Extermination Camp." It was published in the Red Army's newspaper and subsequently broadcast on radio. On August 31, the Russian newspaper *Ogonyok* published an article entitled "Majdanek Death Camp," illustrated with photographs of the crematorium, mass graves, and piles of shoes.

As Soviet reports about Majdanek began circulating around the world, news media from other countries descended on the camp. The first major story in the American press about Majdanek appeared on the front page of the *New York Times* on August 30, 1944, in which journalist W.H. Lawrence offered a chilling eyewitness account of the newly liberated camp (which he called Maidanek):

> I have just seen the most terrible place on the face of the earth—the German concentration camp at Maidanek. . . . I have seen the skeletons of the bodies the Germans did not have time to burn before the Red Army swept into Lublin on July 23, and I have seen evidence such as bone ash still in the furnaces and piled up beside them ready to be taken to near-by fields, on which it was scattered as fertilizer for cabbages. . . . After inspection of Maidanek, I am now prepared to believe any story of German atrocities, no matter how savage, cruel, and depraved.[47]

Although Lawrence was convinced of the reality of Nazi atrocities, most people, especially in the Allied countries, remained unconvinced. BBC correspondent Alexander Werth filed a story about Majdanek, but the radio network refused to air it, calling it a "Russian propaganda stunt."[48] It would take the discovery of other death camps, including the largest and most notorious camp, to finally convince the skeptics of the reality of the Nazi's Final Solution.

Liberating Auschwitz

Documents gathered from Majdanek by intelligence officers gave the Soviets important information about other Nazi camps, including

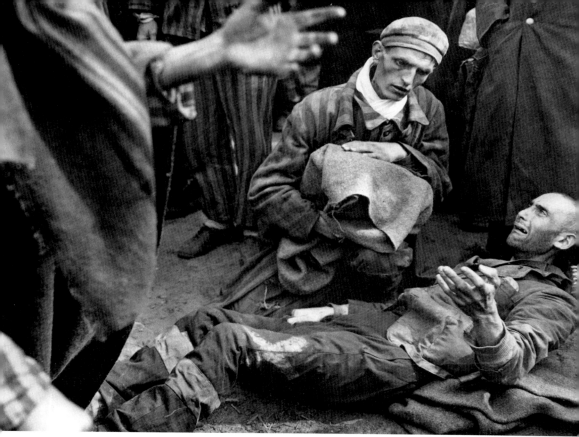

When Soviet troops entered the Majdanek death camp in Poland in 1944 they saw firsthand the gruesome evidence of Hitler's Final Solution. They encountered the crematorium, mass graves, piles of discarded shoes, and desperate prisoners who were, in some cases, barely clinging to life.

the most brutal killing center of all—Auschwitz. This information was sent up the chain of command to high-ranking Soviets, including dictator Joseph Stalin. But the Red Army soldiers in the field had no knowledge of the camp as they advanced through Poland in January 1945. "We bumped into the death camp," explained Lieutenant Vasily Gromadsky. "We had no idea that it was there."[49]

Of the more than twenty thousand camps built by the Nazis, none is more closely associated with the Holocaust than Auschwitz. Established in 1940 for incarcerating Polish political prisoners, Auschwitz rapidly expanded into three main sections—Auschwitz I, a concentration camp; Auschwitz II (Birkenau), an extermination camp; and Auschwitz III (Monowitz), a slave labor camp. Some forty-five subcamps were eventually established around the main camp.

A Russian Soldier at Auschwitz

Twenty-one-year-old Ivan Martynushkin was a senior lieutenant in the Red Army's 332nd Rifle Division when his unit liberated Auschwitz on January 27, 1945. About seven thousand prisoners were left behind when the Nazis abandoned the camp. On many occasions Martynushkin spoke about his feelings as a liberator. Here he recalls his impressions of the survivors at Auschwitz:

It was hard to watch them. I remember their faces, especially their eyes which betrayed their ordeal. . . . At first there was wariness, on both our part and theirs. But then they apparently figured out who we were and began to welcome us, to signal they knew who we were and that we shouldn't be afraid of them—that there were no guards or Germans behind the barbed wire. Only prisoners.

We saw emaciated, tortured, impoverished people. Those were the first people I encountered. . . . We could tell from their eyes that they were happy to be saved from this hell. Happy now that they weren't threatened by death in a crematorium. Happy to be freed. And we had the feeling of doing a good deed—liberating these people from this hell.

Quoted in Ishaan Tharoor, "What a Soviet Soldier Saw When His Unit Liberated Auschwitz 70 Years Ago," *Washington Post*, January 27, 2015. www.washingtonpost.com.

By any measure Auschwitz was the largest and deadliest Holocaust camp. More than 1 million people, the majority of them Jews, died at Auschwitz. Those who did not perish in the gas chambers died of starvation, disease, overwork, or simply being shot by SS guards for any real or imagined infraction of camp rules. One of the most horrific aspects of the camp was the cruel medical experimentation carried out on the prisoners by Dr. Josef Mengele and his staff. Men, women, and even children were subjected to horrifying surgical procedures or excruciating tests in the name of advancing medical science. Few survived the ordeals, which were, in reality, simply another method of murdering innocent people.

Storming the Gates

Unlike at Majdanek, German soldiers remained behind at Auschwitz, mounting a desperate defense as the Red Army approached the camp on January 27, 1945. A fierce battle with retreating German troops left more than two hundred Red Army soldiers dead. When the German guns finally fell silent that afternoon, Soviet troops went through the main entrance of Auschwitz I under a sign that read, *Arbeit Macht Frei* (Work Makes You Free). Sergeant Ivan Sorokopud recalls what he saw inside:

> "After entering the camp [Auschwitz], we saw a dozen 'skeletons.' They moved with considerable difficulty. Through holes in their ragged undergarments we could see their emaciated bodies. The expression 'only skin and bones' was not a figure of speech here but an exact reality."[50]
>
> —Soviet sergeant Ivan Sorokopud.

After entering the camp, we saw a dozen "skeletons." They moved with considerable difficulty. Through holes in their ragged undergarments we could see their emaciated bodies. The expression "only skin and bones" was not a figure of speech here but an exact reality. A putrid odour emanated from these "undead." They were filthy beyond description. Their eyes were huge, and seemed to devour the whole face. . . . They did not speak to us, and made no attempt to talk. They kept at a distance, their eyes darting around. One prisoner, unable to walk, was slowly crawling out of a barracks. Our men stared at him, rooted to the ground.[50]

The Soviet troops next advanced toward Auschwitz-Birkenau, the killing center of the vast camp complex. There they found the rubble of the crematoria, which the fleeing Nazis tried to destroy to hide evidence of their crimes. However, the Nazis could not eradicate

The liberation of the Auschwitz death camp by Soviet troops in 1945 yielded one of many grotesque sights: piles of human hair harvested from murder victims. The Germans planned to use the hair for making coat linings.

all traces of the evidence. In several large storage rooms, the troops found grim reminders of the camp's victims: 836,000 women's coats, 349,000 men's suits, and more than seven tons of human hair.

Among the survivors of Auschwitz were about 180 children who were kept alive and nourished as subjects of Mengele's experiments. Eva Mozes Kor was ten years old when the Soviet troops liberated Auschwitz. "We ran up to them," she recalls, "and they gave us hugs, cookies, and chocolates. Being so alone, a hug meant more than anyone could imagine, because that replaced the human worth we were starving for."[51]

The Soviet liberators found about seven thousand prisoners at Auschwitz, out of about sixty-six thousand inmates tallied at the camp's final roll call in January. The rest had been removed from the camp in one of the most brutal episodes of the Holocaust.

The Auschwitz Death March

By January 1945, with the war virtually lost and the Red Army closing in, the Nazis enacted their plan to relocate the prisoners of Auschwitz to other camps in the west. On January 17, with the sounds of Soviet artillery booming in the distance, the SS began lining up prisoners in columns and marching them out of the camp in the bitter winter weather. Thousands of inmates, already weakened by the rigors of life at Auschwitz, marched through the snow wearing only their thin striped uniforms. The lucky ones had sandals or clogs on their feet. Raizl Kibel, a prisoner and laborer at Auschwitz, recalls the horrific march:

> In a frost, half-barefoot or entirely barefoot, with light rags upon their emaciated and exhausted bodies, tens of thousands of human creatures drag themselves along in the snow. Only the great, strong striving for life, and the light of imminent liberation kept them on their feet.
>
> But woe is to them whose physical strength abandons them. They are shot on the spot. In such a way were thousands who had endured camp life up to the last minute murdered, a moment before liberation.[52]

The shooting of prisoners too weak or sick to keep up occurred with appalling frequency—a grim reality of the death marches. "We started counting the shots," recalls prisoner Aharon Beilin. "It was a long column—five thousand people. We know every shot meant a human life. Sometimes the count reached five hundred, in a single day. And the longer we marched, the more the number of shots increased."[53] Death marches could last for days or weeks. Prisoners on one march endured six weeks of walking through the bitterly cold Polish landscape. Upon arrival at their final destination, only two hundred eighty of the original three thousand marchers had survived the brutal trek.

"We started counting the shots. It was a long column—five thousand people. We know every shot meant a human life. Sometimes the count reached five hundred, in a single day. And the longer we marched, the more the number of shots increased."[53]

—Aharon Beilin, prisoner at Auschwitz.

After the liberation of Auschwitz, the Soviet government estimated the number of deaths at the camp at 4 million. That figure was later revised several times, leading to the present estimate of more than 1 million deaths at Auschwitz.

One Camp After Another

After liberating Auschwitz, the Red Army continued its drive west and in the process encountered one concentration camp after another. Red Army troops reached Gross-Rosen camp on February 13, 1945, shortly after the Nazis forced the camp's remaining forty thousand inmates to embark on a death march. On April 22 Soviets entered the Sachsenhausen concentration camp, finding three thousand prisoners barely alive. Ravensbrück, a women's camp, was liberated on April 29, with about two thousand survivors waiting to be rescued. Stutthof, a camp on the edge of the Baltic Sea, was liberated on May 9, the same day that Germany officially surrendered, ending the war in Europe.

The Soviet Union played a major role in the Allied victory of World War II. Without the tenacious fighting of the Red Army after the invasion by Germany, Hitler's forces might have overrun Europe and won the war. The Soviet liberators who opened the concentration camps in the east, and their American and British counterparts in the west, were the first to view the horrors of the Holocaust camps. Soon the whole world knew of the reality of Jewish genocide by the Nazis and understood the obligation of ensuring that such atrocities will never happen again.

CHAPTER FIVE

Liberation from the West

While the Soviet Red Army was advancing westward through occupied Eastern Europe, other troops of the Allied armies were pushing their way from the west through France. On D-day, June 6, 1944, more than 156,000 American, British, and Canadian troops stormed the beaches of Normandy, France, gaining a foothold on the occupied European continent. Now the Wehrmacht was being squeezed between Allied forces from both the east and the west, a two-front war that Germany could not win. Rapidly advancing through France, the Allies liberated Paris on August 24, 1944.

In March 1945 Allied troops crossed the Rhine River and began the final push through Germany. Despite sporadic offensives launched by the enemy, the Allies encountered little resistance from the retreating German army. In early April soldiers of the US Fourth Armored Division were ordered to search for an underground communications bunker reportedly located in the area. Nearing the small town of Ohrdruf, they discovered something that would affect them for the rest of their lives.

Encountering Horror

As the division's tanks rumbled down the road to Ohrdruf on April 4, Captain Jack Holmes, one of the soldiers in the convoy, observed a bizarre scene:

> We passed by an empty field that had what looked like short pieces of wood sticking out of the ground. The convoy was halted, and we got out to get a closer look at the field. The things sticking out of the ground weren't pieces of wood. They were burned human arms and legs, or what was left of them. The smell of burned and decaying flesh was overwhelming.

Colonel Sears [the commanding officer] got a group of men together to start digging. There were thousands of bodies buried in that field, all in a shallow mass grave, and all of them that still had flesh looked like they had been starved to death.[54]

Continuing along the road, the tanks approached wooden gates leading to several buildings beyond. Tank driver Joe Vanacore pushed the gates open with his tank. "The first thing I saw," he recalls, "was this big pile of bodies, about five, six foot high like a haystack. I didn't realize they were bodies—my mind didn't tell me they were bodies until I got a little closer."[55] Once inside the gates, the men left their tanks and began wandering around the camp, viewing bodies of prisoners lying on the ground, in ditches, or piled up in sheds, and charred corpses stacked on "grills" made of railroad tracks. Four thousand inmates had been murdered before the Allied liberators arrived.

The First Camp

Ohrdruf was the first Nazi camp liberated by the Western Allies. Opened in November 1944, it was a slave-labor subcamp of the infamous Buchenwald concentration camp thirty-two miles (51.5 km) away. In the days before the Fourth Armored's arrival, Ohrdruf's SS guards began marching prisoners to Buchenwald. Those who were unable to make the trek were shot, their bodies left in the camp to be discovered by the Allies. Some prisoners who managed to avoid the death march and execution by hiding in huts and in the surrounding woods were found alive by the liberators. The liberation of Ohrdruf presented irrefutable evidence of Nazi atrocities to the Western Allies.

> "The first thing I saw was this big pile of bodies, about five, six foot high like a haystack. I didn't realize they were bodies—my mind didn't tell me they were bodies until I got a little closer."[55]
>
> —Tank driver Joe Vanacore.

Colonel Hayden Sears, the commander of the Fourth Armored Division, was not content to simply witness the evidence of Nazi atrocities—he wanted ordinary Germans to see what their fellow countrymen had done. A few days after the liberation, local citizens, including Nazi officials, were driven to the camp in the backs

Photographer of the Camps

Photographs played a major role in convincing the American public that the reports of the Nazi atrocities of the Third Reich were indeed true. One of the most famous photojournalists of World War II was Margaret Bourke-White, whose images of the Holocaust camps shocked the world.

Born in 1904 Margaret Bourke-White became interested in photography as a hobby. After making the hobby her profession, she became a photographer for LIFE magazine, with one of her pictures gracing the cover of the magazine's first issue. Bourke-White was the first female war correspondent of World War II, accompanying the US Army into combat zones. In 1945 she toured Buchenwald concentration camp with General George S. Patton, photographing the horrors of the camp in stark black-and-white. "I saw and photographed the piles of naked, lifeless bodies," she recalled, "the human skeletons in furnaces, the living skeletons who would die the next day. . . . Using the camera was almost a relief. It interposed a slight barrier between myself and the horror in front of me."

Bourke-White had a long and distinguished photographic career, documenting everything from steel mills and skyscrapers to Mohandas Gandhi sitting at his spinning wheel. Many of her photographs are now displayed in art museums across the United States. She died of Parkinson's disease in 1971.

Quoted in Editors of LIFE, The Great LIFE Photographers. New York: Little, Brown, 2004, p. 37.

of military trucks. Sears forced the townspeople to walk by the piles of bodies and enter a shed to view the stacked corpses inside. The Germans, well-dressed and holding handkerchiefs over their noses against the stench, betrayed no emotion at the sight of such horror. The Nazis in the group repeatedly muttered that they knew nothing of the atrocities that had occurred at Ohrdruf. Among the civilians who visited the camp were the mayor of the town of Ohrdruf and his wife. A day after their tour, they were found dead in their home—they had hanged themselves.

The Generals Visit Ohrdruf

On April 12 three of the highest-ranking American commanding officers toured Ohrdruf. General Dwight D. Eisenhower, supreme commander of the Allied forces in Europe, was met at the camp by Generals George S. Patton and Omar N. Bradley. Eisenhower had heard disturbing stories about Ohrdruf and was determined to see the camp for himself. Surrounded by American troops and camp survivors, the officers walked among the piles of corpses and burial pits. Eisenhower later sent a report to General George C. Marshall, head of the Joint Chiefs of Staff.

> "I made the visit [to Ohrdruf] deliberately, in order to be in a position to give first-hand evidence of these things if ever, in the future, there develops a tendency to charge these allegations to merely 'propaganda.'"[56]
>
> —General Dwight D. Eisenhower.

The things I saw beggar description. . . . The visual evidence and the verbal testimony of starvation, cruelty, and bestiality were so overpowering as to leave me a bit sick. In one room, where they piled up twenty or thirty naked men, killed by starvation, George Patton would not even enter. He said he would get sick if he did so. I made the visit deliberately, in order to be in a position to give first-hand evidence of these things if ever, in the future, there develops a tendency to charge these allegations to merely "propaganda."[56]

In the weeks to come, more evidence would be uncovered by the advancing Allied troops. Eisenhower made one final announcement before leaving Ohrdruf. "We are told," he said, "that the American soldier does not know what he is fighting for. Now, at least, he will know what he is fighting against."[57]

A Desperate Message

While troops of the Fourth Armored Division were liberating Ohrdruf, inmates in Buchenwald were growing restless. As camp guards learned of the approaching Allies, they began sending thou-

In 1945 General Dwight D. Eisenhower (center) views the bodies of prisoners shot by the Germans at Ohrdruf, a subcamp of the Buchenwald concentration camp. Eisenhower wanted to see for himself the horrors committed by the Nazis so that he could one day give first-hand testimony.

sands of prisoners on forced death marches. A secret underground organization had been established in the camp, and along with their cache of hidden weapons they had a shortwave radio transmitter. On April 8, the day after the evacuations began, the underground leaders sent a frantic message: "To the Allies. To the army of General Patton. This is the Buchenwald concentration camp. SOS. We request help.

They want to evacuate us. The SS wants to destroy us."[58] A few minutes later came the reply: "KZ Bu [concentration camp Buchenwald]. Hold out. Rushing to your aid. Staff of Third Army."[59] The message gave inmates the hope they needed to stage an uprising and await the arrival of the Americans.

Buchenwald, built in 1937 in a forest clearing near Weimar, Germany, held political prisoners, criminals, Roma, Communists, and Jews. The death rate at Buchenwald was high due to forced labor in armament factories, disease, malnutrition, and medical experiments performed by Nazi doctors.

On the morning of April 11 two soldiers of General Patton's Sixth Armored Division on a reconnaissance patrol went through a hole in the barbed-wire fence surrounding Buchenwald. The first Americans to enter the camp, they were greeted by jubilant Communist prisoners who had taken over the camp from the fleeing SS guards. That afternoon more troops and tanks arrived to secure Buchenwald. Me-

Grossly malnourished prisoners at Buchenwald await help after liberation by US troops in 1945. Liberating troops tried to aid the sick and dying as best they could.

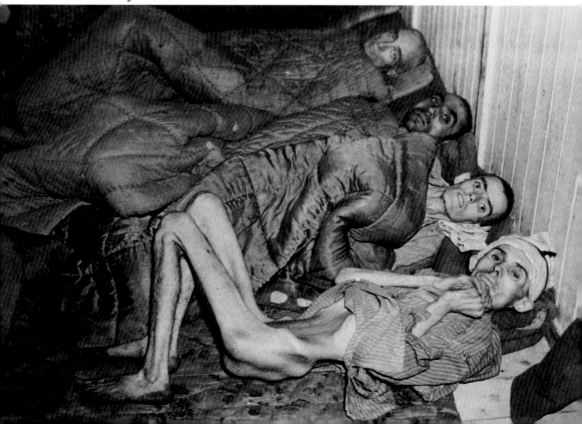

nachem Lipshitz, fourteen years old at the time, was hiding in the camp hospital. He recalls the arrival of US troops:

> When we heard that the Americans were coming, we went on the roof of the hospital, and then I saw American tanks coming from both sides of the camp. A jeep with American soldiers came into the camp, and that's the first time I saw an American soldier in my life. And that's how we were liberated.[60]

The liberating troops found twenty-one thousand prisoners at Buchenwald. The camp was divided into a main camp, where the Communists were held, and a smaller camp filled with Jews, Roma, and others regarded as undesirables. The Communist inmates had been treated fairly well and thus had the strength to overthrow the camp administration. In the small camp, however, the Jews and other prisoners barely survived in overcrowded barracks with little food and medical attention. The most distressing area of the small camp was the children's barracks, where about nine hundred children aged six to fourteen lived in filth.

The 120th Evacuation Hospital, an army medical unit, arrived shortly after the camp was liberated to care for the sick and dying inmates. Bringing in food and medical supplies, the 120th helped those they could, but hundreds still died each day.

Broadcasting the Truth

Edward R. Murrow, the most famous American journalist of World War II, visited Buchenwald on April 12. Renowned for his radio reports from London during the Blitz, Murrow was skeptical of stories hinting at Nazi atrocities. After touring Buchenwald, Murrow went on the air to report on what he had seen, warning his audience of the disturbing report to follow.

> Permit me to tell you what you would have seen and heard had you had been with me on Thursday. It will not be pleasant listening. If you are at lunch, or if you have no appetite to hear what Germans have done, now is a good time to switch off the

radio for I propose to tell you of Buchenwald. . . . There surged around me an evil-smelling stink. Men and boys reached out to touch me. They were in rags and the remnants of uniforms. Death had already marked many of them, but they were smiling with their eyes. . . . We went to the hospital; it was full. The doctor told me that two hundred had died the day before. I asked the cause of death. He shrugged and said: "Tuberculosis, starvation, fatigue, and there are many who have no desire to live. It is very difficult."[61]

An estimated fifty-six thousand inmates perished during the eight years that Buchenwald was operational. After liberating the camp, the Allied soldiers continued their eastward sweep of Nazi Germany, the horrific realities of Hitler's Final Solution becoming clearer with each camp they encountered.

British Liberators

The British army was a major force in World War II, from the first troops coming to France's aid in 1940, through campaigns in North Africa and Italy, to the D-day invasion that liberated Europe. Just as American and Soviet troops had discovered Nazi camps, so did the British army. Just four days after US troops liberated Buchenwald, British and Canadian soldiers encountered the Bergen-Belsen concentration camp, 45 miles (72.4 km) south of Hamburg.

> "There surged around me an evil-smelling stink. Men and boys reached out to touch me. They were in rags and the remnants of uniforms. Death had already marked many of them, but they were smiling with their eyes."[61]
>
> —Newsman Edward R. Murrow.

Bergen-Belsen was divided into subsections for various types of prisoners. These included a detention section where Jews were held for possible exchange for Germans interned in other countries, a section for women, and one for male prisoners too sick to work. Of the one hundred twenty thousand inmates who passed through Bergen-Belsen, more than fifty thousand died from malnutrition and disease. By April 1945 typhus was rampant in the camp, with 500 to 600 prisoners dy-

Witness to Horror

Richard Dimbleby joined the British Broadcasting Corporation (BBC) in 1936, becoming their first war correspondent. He broadcast firsthand reports on battles in North Africa and the D-day invasion. But his most disturbing war broadcast came on April 19, 1945, after he had visited the Bergen-Belsen concentration camp, recently liberated by British troops.

Here over an acre of ground lay dead and dying people. You could not see which was which, except perhaps by a convulsive movement or the last quiver of a sigh from a living skeleton too weak to move. The living lay with their heads against the corpses and around them moved the awful, ghostly procession of emaciated, aimless people, with nothing to do and with no hope of life, unable to move out of your way, unable to look at the terrible sights around them. There was no privacy, nor did men or women ask it any longer. . . .

Babies had been born here, tiny wizened things that could not live. A mother, driven mad, screamed at a British sentry to give her milk for her child, and thrust the tiny mite into his arms, and ran off, crying terribly. He opened the bundle and found the baby had been dead for days.

This day at Belsen was the most horrible of my life.

Quoted in Richard Dimbleby, radio broadcast describing Bergen-Belsen, BBC, April 19, 1945. http://news.bbc.co.uk.

ing of the disease every day. With the danger of typhus spreading to the surrounding area and infecting German civilians and soldiers, on April 12 Bergen-Belsen was surrendered to the advancing British troops.

Lieutenant John Randall was one of the first soldiers to arrive at Bergen-Belsen on April 15, 1945. In a 2005 interview Randall related his first impression as he and his jeep driver entered the camp:

> We were totally unprepared for what we had stumbled across. . . . About 30 yards into the camp, my jeep was suddenly surrounded by a group of about 100 emaciated prisoners. Most of them were in black-and-white striped prison uniforms and the rest wore a terrible assortment of ragged clothes. It was the state of these inmates that made me realise that this was no ordinary PoW camp. . . . They went wild, pleading for food, help, protection and release. I began to get rather alarmed.[62]

A Disturbing Sight

When the main liberating force of British and Canadian troops entered Bergen-Belsen, the true nature of the conditions inside the camp became apparent. About sixty thousand remained in the camp, most of whom were sick or malnourished. Scattered all around the grounds were some thirteen thousand unburied corpses, victims of typhus or starvation. Bodies of men, women, and children were found in mass graves and stacked in piles, some five or six bodies high.

The first priority of the liberators was to properly dispose of the dead. Former SS guards were forced to carry corpses to mass graves for burial, and many contracted and succumbed to typhus. For the inmates who were still alive, desperately needed food and water was brought in by truck. Many soldiers shared their own food with the weakened prisoners. According to one witness, "We gave a bar of chocolate to be divided between three women and they did not have sufficient strength between them to break it into three portions."[63] Often the inmates' weakened digestive systems could not handle the food offered by the British, and many died after eating a simple biscuit.

The disease that permeated the camp was an enormous challenge for the British medical personnel. Doctors and nurses, over-

Under British oversight, former SS guards carry corpses to mass graves at the Bergen-Belsen death camp in 1945. Upon entering the camp, British and Canadian troops encountered stacks of bodies of dead men, women, and children.

worked and understaffed, struggled for two weeks before finally getting the typhus epidemic under control. Despite their heroic work, some thirteen thousand prisoners died after the liberation of Bergen-Belsen.

Aftermath

Once the Bergen-Belsen barracks (or huts) were emptied of prisoners, the liberating forces destroyed the structures. On May 21, 1945, the camp was finally empty and the last building was ready for demolition. A ceremony was held for the liberators and surviving inmates. A British officer addressed the assembled crowd of three hundred.

> In a few moments we are going to burn down the last remaining hut in what was once Belsen concentration camp. . . . It is, I feel, a symbol of the final destruction for all time of the bestial, inhuman creed of Nazi Germany; the creed by which criminals tried to debase the peoples of Europe to serve their own devilish ends. . . . This moment is the end of a chapter, the pages of which are filled with the vilest story of cruelty, hate and bestiality ever written by a nation. You have closed one chapter in the life of some 27,000 final survivors of this camp.[64]

More Holocaust camps were found in the final days of the Third Reich. On April 29 Soviet troops liberated Ravensbrück while US forces liberated Dachau, the Nazis' first concentration camp. The next day, Hitler committed suicide in an underground bunker in Berlin, his dream of world domination shattered by the armies of the Allied nations. Germany officially surrendered on May 8, 1945, to be known as V-E (Victory in Europe) Day. Two days later the last concentration camp, Stutthof, was liberated by the Soviet Red Army.

For the rescuers and liberators of the Holocaust camps, the end of World War II meant the chance to finally go home and resume the lives they had before the war. But those lives would never be quite the same: they were changed by the sights, sounds, and smells of the camps. Many liberators would suffer nightmares for years after their homecoming. They would be hailed as heroes, yet most of them would hesitate to confer that title upon themselves. They were simply people doing what they felt needed to be done.

If the Holocaust changed people, it also changed the world. The cruelties that one human being could inflict on another were laid bare for all to see, especially in the photographs and films that came out of the camps. They were hard to look at, but they presented a truth that needed to be told—a truth that would hopefully prevent another Holocaust from ever happening again.

Introduction: The Courage of the Rescuers

1. Quoted in The History Place, "The Rise of Adolf Hitler: Hitler Named Chancellor." www.historyplace.com.
2. Quoted in Michael W. Perry, ed. *Dachau Liberated: The Official Report by the U.S. Seventh Army Released Within Days of the Camp's Liberation by Elements of the 42ⁿᵈ and 45ᵗʰ Divisions*. Seattle, WA: Inkling, 2000, p. 38.
3. Quoted in Mordecai Paldiel, *The Path of the Righteous: Gentile Rescuers of Jews During the Holocaust*. Hoboken, NJ: KTAV, 1993, p. 379.
4. Dwight D. Eisenhower, *Crusade in Europe*. New York: Doubleday, 1948, p. 408.

Chapter One: Sheltering the Jews

5. Quoted in Mordecai Paldiel, *Sheltering the Jews: Stories of Holocaust Rescuers*. Minneapolis, MN: Augsburg Fortress, 1996, p. 12.
6. Quoted in Corrie ten Boom, Elizabeth Sherrill, and John Sherrill, *The Hiding Place*. Grand Rapids, MI: Chosen, 2006, p. 94.
7. Quoted in ten Boom, Sherrill, and Sherrill, *The Hiding Place*, p. 94.
8. Quoted in Carole C. Carlson, *Corrie ten Boom: Her Life, Her Faith*. Old Tappan, NJ: Revell, 1983, p. 78.
9. Quoted in ten Boom, Sherrill, and Sherrill, *The Hiding Place*, p. 142.
10. Quoted in Paldiel, *The Path of the Righteous*, p. 70.
11. Quoted in Paldiel, *The Path of the Righteous*, p. 71.
12. Quoted in Alex Kershaw, *The Envoy: The Epic Rescue of the Last Jews of Europe in the Closing Months of World War II*. Cambridge, MA: Da Capo, 2010, p. 16.
13. Quoted in Kershaw, *The Envoy*, p. 55.
14. Quoted in Kershaw, *The Envoy*, p. 63.
15. Quoted in Mordecai Paldiel, *The Righteous Among the Nations: Rescuers of Jews During the Holocaust*. Jerusalem: Yad Vashem; New York: HarperCollins, 2007, p. 532.
16. Quoted in Paldiel, *The Righteous Among the Nations*, p. 534.

Chapter Two: Providing a Way Out

17. Quoted in Susan Zuccotti, *Père Marie-Benôit and Jewish Rescue.* Bloomington: Indiana University, 2013, p. 59.
18. Quoted in Paldiel, *The Righteous Among the Nations*, p. 31.
19. Quoted in Paldiel, *The Righteous Among the Nations*, p. 31.
20. Quoted in Zuccotti, *Père Marie-Benôit and Jewish Rescue*, p. 138.
21. Quoted in Paldiel, *The Righteous Among the Nations*, p. 37.
22. Quoted in Maria Julia Cirurgiao and Michael D. Hull, "Aristides de Sousa Mendes," Jewish Virtual Library. www.jewishvirtual library.org.
23. Quoted in Paldiel, *The Righteous Among the Nations*, p. 264.
24. Quoted in Paldiel, *The Righteous Among the Nations*, p. 265.
25. Quoted in Paldiel, *The Path of the Righteous*, p. 60.
26. Quoted in Paldiel, *The Path of the Righteous*, p. 62.
27. Yehuda Bauer, *A History of the Holocaust.* Danbury, CT: Franklin Watts, 2001, p. 249.
28. Quoted in "Nicholas Winton, The Power of Good." www.power ofgood.net.
29. Quoted in "Nicholas Winton, The Power of Good."
30. Quoted in "Nicholas Winton, The Power of Good."
31. Quoted in "Nicholas Winton, The Power of Good."
32. Eva Fogelman, *Conscience and Courage: Rescuers of Jews During the Holocaust.* New York: Anchor, 1994, p. 38.

Chapter Three: Aid and Rescue Groups

33. Quoted in Renée Poznanski, Nathan Bracher, Trans., *Jews in France During World War II.* Hanover, NH: Brandeis University, 2001, p. 191.
34. Quoted in "1,200 Jewish Children of Deported Mothers Will Be Evacuated from Paris by JDC," JTA, August 30, 1942. www.jta .org.
35. Quoted in "1,200 Jewish Children of Deported Mothers Will Be Evacuated from Paris by JDC," JTA.
36. Quoted in Sarah A. Ogilvie and Scott Miller, *Refuge Denied: The St. Louis Passengers and the Holocaust.* Madison: University of Wisconsin, 2006, p. 23.

37. Quoted in Henning Mielke, "Quakers in Germany During and After the World Wars," *Friends Journal*, April 1, 2010. www.friendsjournal.org.

38. Alice Resch Synnestvedt, *Over the Highest Mountains: A Memoir of Unexpected Heroism in France During World War II.* Pasadena, CA: Intentional Productions, 2005, pp. 127, 128.

39. Quoted in Mielke, "Quakers in Germany During and After the World Wars."

40. Quoted in Paldiel, *The Path of the Righteous*, p. 469.

41. Quoted in "Paula Zahn Interviews Nelly Trocmé Hewett, Hanne Liebmann and Pierre Sauvage," *CBS This Morning*, April 24, 1990. www.chambon.org.

Chapter Four: Liberation from the East

42. Quoted in Michael Jones, *Total War: From Stalingrad to Berlin.* London: John Murray, 2011, p. 160.

43. Joshua Rubenstein, "What They Saw: The Liberation of Majdanek 70 Years Ago Today," WBUR, July 23, 2014. www.cognoscenti.wbur.org.

44. Quoted in Jones, *Total War*, p. 160.

45. Quoted in *Time*, "Poland: Vernichtungslager," August 24, 1944. http://time.com.

46. Quoted in Jones, *Total War*, p. 161.

47. W.H. Lawrence, "Nazi Mass Killing Laid Bare in Camp," *New York Times*, August 30, 1944. www.scribd.com.

48. Alexander Werth, *Russia at War, 1941–1945.* New York: Carroll & Graf, 1984, p. 890.

49. Quoted in Jones, *Total War*, p. 183.

50. Quoted in Jones, *Total War*, p. 195.

51. Quoted in Laurence Rees, *Auschwitz: A New History.* New York: PublicAffairs, 2005, p. 260.

52. Quoted in Martin Gilbert, *The Holocaust: A History of the Jews of Europe During the Second World War.* New York: Holt, Rinehart and Winston, 1985, p. 775.

53. Quoted in Gilbert, *The Holocaust*, p. 775.

Chapter Five: Liberation from the West

54. Quoted in "There Were Bodies Everywhere: Jack Holmes' Memory of Ohrdruf." www.captainjackholmes.weebly.com.

55. Quoted in Michael Hirsch, *The Liberators: America's Witnesses to the Holocaust*. New York: Bantam, 2010, p. 27.

56. Quoted in Hirsch, *The Liberators*, p. 101.

57. Quoted in Hirsch, *The Liberators*, p. 100.

58. Quoted in Ian Buruma, *Year Zero: A History of 1945*. New York: Penguin, 2013, p. 242.

59. Quoted in Buruma, *Year Zero*, p. 242.

60. Quoted in Hirsch, *The Liberators*, p. 43.

61. "Ed Murrow Reports from Buchenwald—April 15, 1945." www.library.berkeley.edu.

62. Quoted in Alexander van Straubenzee, "The Gates of Hell," *Telegraph*, April 10, 2005. www.telegraph.co.uk.

63. Quoted in Joanne Reilly, *Belsen: The Liberation of a Camp*. London: Routledge, 1998, p. 26.

64. Quoted in Jon Bridgman, *The End of the Holocaust: The Liberation of the Camps*. Portland, OR: Areopagitica, 1990, pp. 55–56.

Joseph André

A Catholic priest posted to a parish in Namur, Belgium, André secured safe havens for Jewish children during the Holocaust. After World War II, André procured permanent living arrangements for the children he had rescued.

Père Marie-Benôit

A Capuchin monk of the Roman Catholic Church, Benôit produced false identity cards that allowed French Jews to emigrate to safety in neutral countries. He was known as "Father of the Jews" for his heroic actions.

Cornelia "Corrie" ten Boom

When the Nazis occupied the Netherlands, ten Boom sheltered Jews in a secret room in "Beje," her home in Amsterdam. She was arrested and spent almost four months at Ravensbrück concentration camp. Upon her release, ten Boom established a rehabilitation center for Holocaust survivors.

Adolf Eichmann

Eichmann was an SS Lieutenant Colonel and head of the Gestapo's Department of Jewish Affairs. He coordinated the relocation of European Jews to the Holocaust camps.

Dwight D. Eisenhower

Supreme Commander of the Allied Forces in Europe, General Eisenhower masterminded the June 6, 1944, D-day invasion. The massive operation opened up the Western front in Europe, liberating France and ensuring Germany's ultimate defeat.

Adolf Hitler

Founder of the Nazi Party and chancellor of Germany from 1933 to 1945. An anti-Semite, his plan to create an Aryan "Master Race" led to the Holocaust and the extermination of 6 million Jews.

Aristides de Sousa Mendes

The Portuguese consul general of Bordeaux, France, Mendes disregarded orders from his superiors and distributed visas allowing Jewish refugees to live in neutral Portugal. For his defiance, Mendes was relieved from his post and died in poverty.

André Trocmé

Pastor of the Protestant church in the French village of Le Chambon-sur-Lignon, Trocmé inspired his congregation to provide safe havens for persecuted Jews, saving some five thousand lives.

Raoul Wallenberg

A Swedish diplomat who saved tens of thousands of Hungarian Jews by issuing official-looking but illegal identity papers called Schutz-passes. Arrested by the Soviets in 1945, Wallenberg disappeared and was never seen again.

Nicholas Winton

Operating out of a hotel room while on vacation in Prague, Czechoslovakia, Winton organized a massive rescue operation, transporting 669 Jewish children to safety in England. Some five thousand descendants of those children proudly call themselves "Winton's Children."

Books

Richard Bessel, *Germany 1945: From War to Peace*. New York: HarperCollins, 2010.

Daniel Blatman, *The Death Marches: The Final Phase of Nazi Genocide*. Cambridge, MA: Harvard University, 2011.

Corrie ten Boom, Elizabeth Sherrill, and John Sherrill, *The Hiding Place*. Grand Rapids, MI: Chosen, 2006.

Louise W. Borden, *His Name Was Raoul Wallenberg: Courage, Rescue, and Mystery During World War II*. New York: HMH, 2012.

David M. Crowe, *The Holocaust: Roots, History, and Aftermath*. Boulder, CO: Westview, 2008.

Michael Hirsh, *The Liberators*. New York: Bantam, 2010.

Ian Kershaw, *The End: The Defiance and Destruction of Hitler's Germany, 1944–1945*. New York: Penguin, 2011.

Caroline Moorehead, *Village of Secrets: Defying the Nazis in Vichy, France*. New York: HarperCollins, 2014.

Steven Pressman, *50 Children: One Ordinary Couple's Extraordinary Rescue Mission into the Heart of Nazi Germany*. New York: Harper Perennial, 2015.

Dan Stone, *The Liberation of the Camps: The End of the Holocaust and Its Aftermath*. New Haven, CT: Yale University, 2015.

Internet Sources

"Corrie ten Boom House Virtual Tour." http://tenboom.com/en.

Egon W. Fleck, "Buchenwald: A Preliminary Report." http://contentdm.warwick.ac.uk/cdm/ref/collection/tav/id/1348.

"Nicholas Winton, The Power of Good." http://www.powerofgood.net/story.php.

Ishaan Tharoor, "What a Soviet Soldier Saw When His Unit Liberated Auschwitz 70 Years Ago." http://www.washingtonpost.com/blogs/worldviews/wp/2015/01/27/what-a-soviet-soldier-saw-when-his-unit-liberated-auschwitz-70-years-ago.

Websites

American Jewish Joint Distribution Committee (www.jdc.org). This website presents a complete story of the JDC's relief work from its inception to the present day. Includes archives, photographs, and an interactive history of the organization.

Holocaust Chronicle (www.holocaustchronicle.org). An in-depth website with information on all aspects of the Holocaust, searchable by keyword. Includes numerous photographs and a Holocaust timeline.

Teacher's Guide to the Holocaust (http://fcit.coedu.usf.edu/holocaust/default.htm). A comprehensive guide to all aspects of the Holocaust. Includes a timeline, articles, and numerous links to firsthand accounts by victims, rescuers, children, liberators, and more.

US Holocaust Memorial Museum (www.ushmm.org). A comprehensive guide to the Holocaust, including articles, photographs, films, survivor accounts, and information about the museum in Washington, DC.

Yad Vashem (www.yadvashem.org). Contains a list of non-Jews honored as Righteous Among the Nations since 1963. Among many other features are a searchable database of Holocaust victims, a photo archive, and a resource center with in-depth information about the Holocaust.

INDEX

PICTURE CREDITS

Cover: © Corbis

Maury Aaseng, 8

Album/Document/Newscom, 61

© Dave Bartruff/Corbis, 13

© Bettmann/Corbis, 27, 39, 62

British soldiers oversee the clearing of bodies at Bergen-Belsen death camp by former SS guards following German defeat, Bergen-Belsen, 1945 (b/w photo), German Photographer (20th Century)/© SZ Photo/Bridgeman Images, 67

© Corbis, 17

© Peter Langer/Design Pics/Corbis, 54

Mondadori/Newscom, 51

SA March in Dortmund, 1933, from 'Germany Awakened' (colour litho), German School (20th century)/Private Collection/The Stapleton Collection/Bridgeman Images, 23

Alex Segre/REX, 20

Shutterstock, 31, 34, 41

Thinkstock Images, 4, 5

Two Wehrmacht soldiers are attacking a bunker on the Eastern Front in Russia, 1941 (photo), German Photographer, (20th century)/© Galerie Bilderwelt/Bridgeman Images, 47